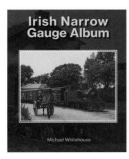
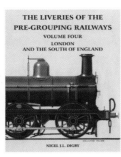
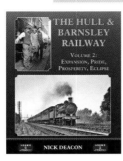
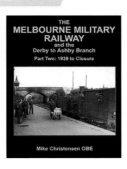

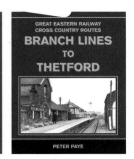

RAILWAY TITLES

BRITISH RAILWAY HISTORY IN COLOUR SERIES

Vol. 1: West Gloucester and Wye Valley Lines (2nd Ed.)	£30.00 .....
Vol. 2: Forest of Dean Lines and the Severn Bridge	OOP .....
Vol. 3: Gloucester Midland Lines Part 1: North	£30.00 .....
Vol. 4A: Gloucester Midland Lines Part 2: South	£25.00 .....
Vol. 4B: Gloucester Midland Lines Part 3: South	£30.00 ....
Vol. 5: Gloucester to Swindon & Branches	TBA ....
Vol. 8: Warwicks Western Region Lines 1 (due Jan. 2021)	£30.00 ....
Supplement to West Gloucester and Wye Valley Lines	£7.50 .....

BRITISH RAILWAYS THE FIRST 25 YEARS SERIES

Vol. 1: East Midlands	OOP .....
Vol. 2: West Midlands	£25.00 .....
Vol. 3: North West. Lancashire & Westmoreland	£25.00 .....
Vol. 4: South West. Somerset & Devon	£25.00 .....
Vol. 5: South West. N Devon, Plymouth & Cornwall	OOP .....
Vol. 6: Central London. Southern Region	£22.50 .....
Vol. 7: London. Western Region	£22.50 .....
Vol. 8: North East	£22.50 .....
Vol. 9: London. LMR & LTSR Region	£22.50 .....
Vol. 10: Mid Wales, Cambrian Coast & NG Lines	£22.50 .....

ENGLISH RAILWAYS

Aspects of Southern Steam	£25.00 .....
Banbury & Cheltenham Direct Railway	£24.99 .....
Biddulph Valley Line Vol. 1	TBA .....
Branch Lines to Maldon	£30.00 .....
Branch Lines to Thetford	£30.00 .....
British Carriage & Wagon Builders & Repairers (2nd Ed.)	£30.00 .....
Broad Gauge Engines of the GWR Pt 1 1837-40	£22.50 .....
Broad Gauge Engines of the GWR Pt 2 1840-45	£22.50 .....
Broad Gauge Railway at Watchet	£9.00 .....
BR Steam in Dean	£10.00 .....
Chard Branch	£35.00 .....

Colonel Stephens and his Railmotors	£22.50 .....
Crystal Palace High Level Railway	£15.00 .....
East Somerset & Cheddar Valley Railways	£30.00 .....
Golden Age of London's Railways from Old Postcards	£25.00 .....
Gone To War: The NSR's Fallen Railwaymen	£25.00 .....
Gorton Tank: A History of Gorton Works	TBA .....
Great Northern Branch Lines From Stamford	£25.00 .....
Great Western Steam 1934-49	£22.50 .....
GWR Structure Colours 1912-1947 (GWSG)	£14.95 .....
Harecastle's Canal & Railway Tunnels	£25.00 .....
Hull & Barnsley Railway Vol. 1	£25.00 .....
Hull & Barnsley Railway Vol. 2	£35.00 .....
LB&SCR: The Bennett Collection	£19.95 .....
Liveries of Pre-Group Railways Vol. 1 West & Wales	£12.00 .....
Liveries of Pre-Group Railways Vol. 2 NE & Scot.	£12.00 .....
Liveries of Pre-Group Railways Vol. 3 North & Scot.	£15.00 .....
Liveries of Pre-Group Railways Vol. 4 London & South	£15.00 .....
Mainline to Industry	£9.95 .....
Minehead Branch (2nd Ed.)	£24.99 .....
Monorails of the 19th Century	£24.99 .....
Monorails of the Early 20th Century	£25.00 .....
Motor Rail Catalogues	£24.00 .....
North Staffordshire in LM&SR Days Vol 3	£25.00 .....
Red Panniers	£27.00 .....
Robinson's Locomotive Liveries on the GCR	£19.50 .....
Saltney Carriage & Wagon Works (GWSG)	£12.75 .....
Severn & Wye Railway Vol. 5: Lydney Docks	£25.00 .....
Shrewsbury & Welshpool Railway	£12.00 .....
Somerset & Dorset Railway 1935-1966	£25.00 .....
South Eastern & Chatham Railway Carriages★★	£19.95 .....
Stafford & Uttoxeter Railway	£30.00 .....
Stations & Structures M&GNJR Vol. 1 (East section)	OOP .....
Stations & Structures M&GNJR Vol. 2 (West section)	£30.00 .....
Stratford & Midland Junction Railway Vol. 1	£25.00 .....
Stratford & Midland Junction Railway Vol. 2	£35.00 .....

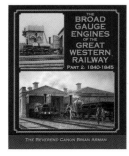
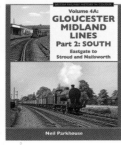
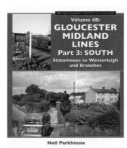
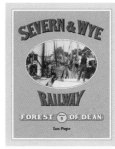
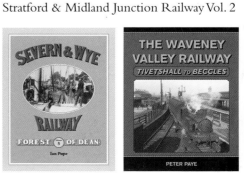
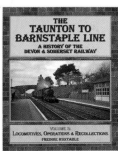

  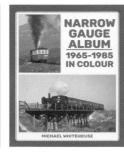 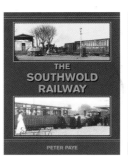  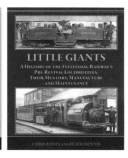

Taunton to Barnstaple Line Vol. 1: History	£25.00	Great North of Scotland Railway Carriages	£19.95 .....
Taunton to Barnstaple Line Vol. 2: The Route, etc	£25.00	Haymarket Motive Power Depot★★	£24.99 .....
Taunton to Barnstaple Line Vol. 3: Operating, etc	£25.00	Montrose & Bervie Railway	£25.00 .....
The Knotty: An Illustrated Survey of the NSR	£14.95	More on Caledonian Wagons: A Supplement	£10.00 .....
Waveney Valley Railway: Tivetshall to Beccles	£30.00	Operating the Caledonian Railway Vol. 1	£22.50 .....
Western Region Steam 1950-65★★	£22.50	Operating the Caledonian Railway Vol. 2	£25.00 .....
Wirral Railway & Its Predecessors	£24.99	Paisley & Barrhead District Railway	£15.00 .....
		Port Road	£30.00 .....

MILITARY RAILWAYS

		Scottish Shale Oil Industry & Mineral Railway Lines	£25.00 .....
Beachley and the First World War	£25.00	Signalling the Caledonian Railway	£30.00 .....
Longmoor Military Railway Vol. 1: 1903-39	OOP	Vanished Railways of West Lothian	£25.00 .....
Longmoor Military Railway Vol. 2: 1939-60	OOP	William Pickersgill and the '956' Class Locos	£25.00 .....
Longmoor Military Railway Vol. 3: Closure & Stock	£30.00		
Melbourne Military Railway Vol. 1	£25.00		

WELSH RAILWAYS

Melbourne Military Railway Vol. 2	£35.00	A North Wales Travelogue	£10.00 .....
Shrops & Monts Railway Under Military Control	£22.50	Bala Branch	£25.00 .....
		Ifor Higgon's Cambrian Diary	£10.00 .....

NARROW GAUGE RAILWAYS

		Llanelly Railway & Dock Company (WV)	£22.50 .....
Cliffe Hill Mineral Railway (PP)	£9.95	Port Talbot Railway & Docks Vol. 1: 1853-1907	£25.00 .....
First Hundred Locomotives From Alan Keef Ltd	TBA	Port Talbot Railway & Docks Vol. 2: 1894-1971	£30.00 .....
Industrial Narrow Gauge Album (h/b) (PP)	£25.95	Rhymney Railway Drawings	£18.00 .....
Industrial Narrow Gauge Album (s/b) (PP)	£19.95	Ruabon to Barmouth Line	OOP .....
Irish Narrow Gauge Album	£25.00	Swansea Vale Railway: A Midland Outpost	£30.00 .....
Little Giants: History Festiniog Rly's Pre-Revival Locos	£60.00		

FOREIGN RAILWAYS

Narrow Gauge Album 1950-1965 In Colour	£25.00		
Narrow Gauge Album 1965-1985 In Colour	£25.00	Austrian Narrow Gauge	£15.00 .....
Reservoir Builders of South Wales (PP)	£14.95	A Contrast in Islands (Corsica & Sardinia) (PP)★	£27.95 .....
Ruston & Hornsby Diesel Locomotive Album (PP)	£28.00	Early Years Motor Rail & Tram Car Co 1911-31 (PP)	£19.95 .....
Simplex Locomotives at Work	£15.00	Fortress Railways of the Baltic Shores (PP)★	£8.95 .....
Southwold Railway	£25.00	Indian Metre Gauge Steam (PP)	£19.95 .....
Tralee & Dingle Railway	TBA	Light Railway Construction (PP)	£4.95 .....
		Light Railway Railcar in Western Europe (PP)	£29.95 .....
		Narrow Gauge by the Sudanese Red Sea Coast (PP)	£5.95 .....

SCOTTISH RAILWAYS

		Rails Through Majorca (PP)	£21.95 .....
Branch Lines of Strathearn	£30.00	Railways of the Andes (PP)	£21.95 .....
Caledonian Railway Carriages	£30.00		

PRIVATE OWNER WAGONS SERIES

Caledonian Railway 'Jumbos'★★	£22.50		
Caledonian Railway Locomotives: The Formative Years	£35.00	Private Owner Wagons: A First Collection	OOP .....
Caledonian Railway Locomotives: The Classic Years	£35.00	Private Owner Wagons: A Second Collection	OOP .....
Caledonian Railway Wagons	£30.00	Private Owner Wagons: A Third Collection	OOP .....
Caledonian Railway's Wemyss Bay Station	£5.00	Private Owner Wagons: A Fourth Collection	£19.95 .....
Cathcart Circle	£22.50	Private Owner Wagons: A Fifth Collection	£19.95 .....
Dalry Road MPD, Edinburgh 1848-1965	£25.00	Private Owner Wagons: A Sixth Collection	£21.00 .....
Edinburgh St. Margaret's: The 'Other' NBR Shed	£30.00		

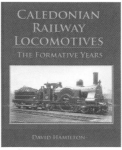 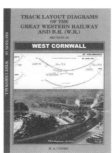 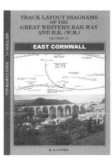 

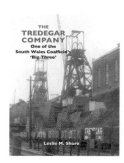   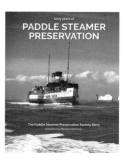 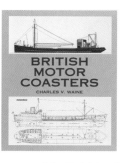 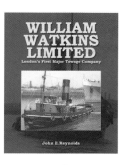

Private Owner Wagons: A Seventh Collection	£19.95	Ferries & Pleasure Steamers of the British Isles	£25.00 .....
Private Owner Wagons: An Eighth Collection	OOP	Foxton Inclined Plane	£22.50 .....
Private Owner Wagons: A Ninth Collection	£19.95	Gloucester Docks An Historical Guide	£5.00 .....
Private Owner Wagons: A Tenth Collection	£21.00	Harecastle's Canal & Railway Tunnels	£25.00 .....
Private Owner Wagons: An Eleventh Collection	£21.00	Irish Sea Schooner Twilight	£24.99 .....
Private Owner Wagons: A Twelfth Collection	£21.00	James Smart of Chalford	£18.00 .....
Private Owner Wagons: A Thirteenth Collection	£22.50	Mersey Ferries Vol. 2 Wallasey Ferries★★	£20.00 .....
Private Owner Wagons: A Fourteenth Collection	£22.50	Severn Traders	£26.95 .....
Private Owner Wagons: A Fifteenth Collection	£22.50	Glamorganshire and Aberdare Canals Vol. 1	£30.00 .....
Private Owner Wagons of Bristol	£18.00	Glamorganshire and Aberdare Canals Vol. 2	£30.00 .....
Private Owner Wagons of Gloucestershire★★	£21.99	Paddle Steamer Preservation: Sixty Years of the PSPS	£25.00 .....
Private Owner Wagons of Somerset	£25.00	Port of Penzance	£4.99 .....
Private Owner Wagons of the Forest of Dean	OOP	'Tin Boats' of the Royal Airforce Marine Branch	TBA .....
Private Owner Wagons of the South-East	£22.50	Trent & Mersey Canal: Trade & Transport 1770-1970	£25.00 .....
		Vickers' Master Shipbuilder	£24.99 .....
		Wigan Pier	£9.99 .....

TRACK LAYOUT DIAGRAMS

10	West Cornwall	£8.00 .....
11	East Cornwall	£10.00 .....
19A	Bristol Area	£8.00 .....
29	Stratford & Midland Junction Rly	£5.00 .....
36	Ross, Monmouth & Chepstow	£7.00 .....
37	Forest of Dean	£8.00 .....
43A	Cardiff (GWR) Main Line	£8.00 .....
43B	Cardiff Docks	£9.00 .....
45	Caerphilly	TBA .....
46A	Rhondda Valleys	£7.50 .....
46B	Pontypridd to Cardiff	£7.50 .....
52	Neath & Brecon Railway	£6.00 .....
59	Central Wales	£6.00 .....
60	Aberystwyth to Welshpool	£6.00 .....

William Watkins Ltd (Tugs & Towage) £25.00 .....

INDUSTRIAL & MINING

A World Gone By: E.B. Taylor of Witney	£13.50 .....
Chester Lead Works	£25.00 .....
Coal From Camerton	£15.00 .....
Digging Bath Stone	TBA .....
Engine Houses of West Cornwall	£18.00 .....
Engine Houses of Mid Cornwall	£18.00 .....
Engine Houses of East Cornwall	TBA .....
From the Mendips to the Sea	£15.00 .....
Fuller's Earth Mining Industry Around Bath	£15.00 .....
Gazetteer of Coal Mines of S Wales & Monmouthshire	£30.00 .....
History of Thomas Green Ltd★	£18.00 .....
Industrial Gwynedd Vol. 3 (PP)	£6.00 .....
North Staffordshire Collieries at Chell	£7.50 .....
Peerless Powell Dyffryn	£24.99 .....
Tredegar Coal & Iron Co. Ltd	£25.00 .....
Waller's Description of the Mines in Cardiganshire★	£9.99 .....

THE FOREST RAILWAY STORIES SERIES

1: Counting Sheep	£5.00 .....
2: Teddy's Christmas	£5.00 .....
3: Mr Thistle's Whistle	£5.00 .....

MARITIME & CANAL

A Glance Back at Lydney Docks	OOP .....
A Guide to the Anderton Boat Lift	£5.00 .....
Anderton Boat Lift	£22.50 .....
Balmoral and the Bristol Channel	£22.50 .....
British Motor Coasters	£25.00 .....
British Motor Trawlers Vol. 1	£30.00 .....
British Steam Trawlers	£30.00 .....
Cosens of Weymouth 1848-1918★★	£29.95 .....

FOREST OF DEAN LOCAL HISTORY

A Glance Back at Mitcheldean	£4.50 .....
All Hands to the Pumps (Fountain Inn, Parkend)	£7.50 .....
Bermuda Dick	£12.95 .....
Blood on Coal	OOP .....
Cinderford St. John's Cricket Club	£5.00 .....
Cottrell's Coaches of Mitcheldean	£12.75 .....

  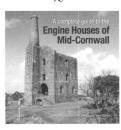 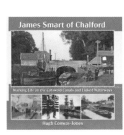 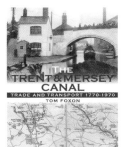 

Edwardian Dean	£7.50 .....
Old Stone Crosses of West Gloucestershire	£4.95 .....
Overlooking the Wye	£7.50 .....
Parkend. A Forest of Dean Village	£9.99 .....
Retrieving Wenty's Sturty Bird	£11.99 .....
Robert Mushet and the Darkhill Ironworks	£7.99 .....
The Commoners of Dean Forest★	£24.99 .....
The Free Miners of the Forest of Dean★★	£36.00 .....
The Verderers and Forest Laws of Dean★	£24.99 .....
Tradition, Reformation & Reaction in Dean 1450–1603	£15.00 .....

FACSIMILE SERIES

A Treatise on Forest of Dean Stone 1913	£4.50 .....
Dock Developments at Newport, 1907	£4.95 .....
Fine Forest Coal c1930	OOP .....
Lydney Harbour Dues & Regulations, 1902	£3.95 .....

ARCHIVE

Issues 1–20 each (*2,9,11 & 15 sold out, 6 & 12*★★)	£5.00 .....
Issues 21–66 each (*23 sold out, 22 & 26*★★)	£6.00 .....
Issues 66–97 each	£6.75 .....
Issues 98–108 each	£7.50 .....

The Journal for British Industrial & Transport History.
Quarterly. Published March, June, September, December.

RAILWAY ARCHIVE

Issues 1–27 each (*1,5,10-13,16,19,20, 27 sold out* – rest ★★)	£7.50 .....

Issues 28–48 each (*29 sold out, 30, 33, 36*★★)	£8.25 .....
Issues 49–50 each (*50 sold out*)	£9.75 .....

Publication ceased with No. 50. A full list of the articles in every issue of both **Archive** and **Railway Archive** is available on the website as a downloadable PDF file or write enclosing an sae.

NOTES:

★ Stocks of these titles are low.
★★ Stocks of these titles are in single figures.
OOP – Out of print
TBA – Price to be announced. Titles in production, publication expected in the next 6 months.
PP – Plateway Press. We have bought the entire stock of this quality publisher specialising in narrow gauge, industrial & foreign railway titles
GWSG – Great Western Study Group – we hold stocks of these titles which we can also supply on trade terms
WV – Wider View – we have the remaining stock of this title

Irish Narrow Gauge Album

Listowel & Ballybunion: One railway which never survived the 'Troubles' was the famous Listowel & Ballybunion, which closed permanently in 1924. As a monorail, it can hardly be described as a narrow gauge line. It was built in 1877 without Government assistance and opened on leap year day, 29th February, 1888, mainly as a showcase demonstration nine miles long of the practical possibilities of the Lartigue system. Unfortunately a sales pitch addressed to the rest of the world from one of the remoter corners of County Kerry suffered from a certain degree of inaudibility. But, all the same, the Ballybunion line, aided no doubt by its mere name, shines brightly in Irish railway legend and eclipses many more important railways which operated much more recently. This view is at Listowel station.

Previous page: The County Donegal Railway Joint Committee had sizeable workshops at Stranorlar and the rolling stock was maintained here. One of the 1893 built carriages is seen on 22nd August, 1956 jacked up off its bogies having what looks like a new buffer headstock fitted. The tank for the acetylene lighting can be seen on the end of the carriage which was charged from the workshop. Carriage No. 38 stands in the background.
[Photo: Pat Whitehouse]

LARTIGUE RAILWAY. LISTOWEL. Co.KERRY. 9841. W.L

Irish Narrow Gauge Album

Michael Whitehouse

Cavan & Leitrim 4-4-0T *Lady Edith* beginning her preserved life having been bought for transhipment to the USA by Edgar T. Mead. Ironically, she follows in the footsteps of many Irishmen who also emigrated.

Acknowledgements

The pictures in this book are all from my own collection, previously my father's. I have attributed the photographer or the holder of the image where known; but, even so, there are conflicts. In researching some of the captions I have seen that in other books, the same image is credited to someone else; this may be right but, on the other hand, it is also eminently likely that several people took the same image simultaneously by joining together on the same excursion. I have not been able to trace many of the photographers as most have now gone to that engine shed in the sky.

I have received the willing assistance of several friends in checking the text and images where it is possible to do so. Simon Star and David Pinniger have checked the captions. The *Railway Magazine* consented to the use of articles contemporary to some of the images. *The National Library*, Dublin provided 'PBW' with several early prints from the glass plates of the Lawrence Collection and the *National Railway Museum* agreed to my using several photographs taken by A.W. Croughton which my father saved originally and transferred to the national collection for posterity. Particularly, I would like to thank my mother who has diligently read the whole book in typed form and suggested corrections. Of course, she remembers most of these railways first hand too, having accompanied my father to see the dying embers, enjoying the experience and sharing some excellent meals in the Irish hotels at the time.

About the Author

Michael Whitehouse has always been interested in narrow gauge railways. Having been brought up intrinsically to know railways inside and out, he has enjoyed accompanying 'PBW' searching out railways worldwide and still continues to do so, even to the far reaches of South America, South East Asia and China. Being given his own camera at the age of ten which he has continued to upgrade, he has very many railway pictures which, when added to 'PBW's' collection, range into their thousands.

Since his early twenties, Michael has been involved in running narrow gauge railways in Wales. First, volunteering at Boston Lodge in his university days on the Festiniog Railway, then firing on the Welshpool & Llanfair Railway, he then stepped up to volunteering his time as a lawyer to assist the regeneration of the Welsh Highland Railway, finally becoming Chairman of the Festiniog Railway Company itself. In his career as a project finance lawyer, Michael has also been involved in narrow gauge railways: advising International Finance Corporation and the Governments of Kenya and Uganda on concessioning the metre gauge East Africa Railway and also, working with South African banks on the privatisation of the Cape Gauge Zambia Railway which leads to the world famous Victoria Falls bridge.

Contents

Published by
LIGHTMOOR PRESS
© Lightmoor Press & Michael Whitehouse 2020
British Library Cataloguing-in-Publication Data.
A catalogue record for this book is available from the British Library
ISBN: 97819038 81 8

LIGHTMOOR PRESS
Unit 144B, Harbour Road Trading Estate, Lydney, Gloucestershire GL15 4EJ
www.lightmoor.co.uk / info@lightmoor.co.uk
Lightmoor Press is an imprint of Black Dwarf Lightmoor Publications Ltd
Printed in Poland
www.lfbookservices.co.uk

Clogher Valley Tramway: Ireland had many narrow gauge railways which ran alongside the road and followed its undulations, largely because most such lines were cheaply built and so they had little option. The Clogher Valley Tramway issued a glowing prospectus but completely failed to live up to its expectations. The tramway was largely run by a fleet of six Sharp Stewart built 0-4-2Ts with the regulation 'skirts' hiding the wheels and motion so as not to scare horses and other animals.

Introduction

"The state of Ireland is one which is notorious. Ireland is our disgrace"
[Lord Grey, House of Lords, 23rd March, 1846]

In order to understand the context for the Irish narrow gauge railways, it is first necessary to explain a little of the complex history of Ireland itself. Usually, history is written by the victorious, but that is often not the whole story. By the 19th century, Ireland had become a thorn in the side of England.

History shows us what can happen when a country has no government of its own and is obliged to rely on another. For many centuries, the English had plundered Ireland and mistreated both the country and its people. In 1800, the Act of Union subsumed Ireland into the United Kingdom. Soon after, Irish overreliance on potatoes as the staple diet severely added to the country's problems, following multiple crop blights in the 1840s.

If that was not enough, Irish trade had been severely taxed over the years, especially when it competed with English trading or military interests. Power was concentrated in London. But the Irish Celtic spirit was undiminished and fuelled by evangelists and catholic taunting. Secret societies emerged as a result of local grievances. These were to lay deep foundations for dissent.

Many Irish had emigrated to America, creating a massive diaspora who supported moves for Irish independence, and assisting the 1916 Easter Rising and the subsequent foundation of the IRA. Such support continued at least up to Tony Blair's 1997 apology for the famine and the conclusion of the Good Friday Agreement of 1998.

A Royal Commission had been set up to look at the Irish situation as long ago as 1833 under Richard Whately, the Protestant Archbishop of Dublin. The Commission recommended economic regeneration which eventually led to the creation of railways, particularly to open up remote districts, but the processes established were bureaucratic and cumbersome, designed as far as possible to minimise cost. A region seeking assistance had to begin the process by sending a petition to the Lord Lieutenant, which was then forwarded to relief commissioners and the Board of Works for inspection. Next it was sent to a local surveyor who prepared a report on the validity of the scheme for the Board of Works which, if it accepted the surveyor's findings, then made a recommendation back to the Lord Lieutenant, who then sought permission from where it counted: the Treasury. The government would advance loans to enable the works to be carried out, but the money had to be repaid by the counties where the works took place. Many of the railways illustrated in the book were built pursuant to this process, which often resulted in a railway built too cheaply and without adequate governance in its approval. Such cumbersome process was to lead to infamous events and accidents, and also made the railways notorious both locally and with ferro equinologists.

I am lucky enough to have met some Irish folk who remember the Irish narrow gauge railways and to hear their stories: an 82-year-old farmer sitting at Fitzgerald's bar at Castlegregory, with his feet on original Tralee & Dingle rail used as a foot stool, remembered the train when he took his cattle to Dingle fair. He also recalled with some glee the day he won 20:1 at Cheltenham races which kept him in Guinness for two years! At Camp bridge, 93-year-old Michael O'Shea and his wife, Mary, lived in the small stone house next to the river where the worst railway disaster on the Tralee & Dingle Railway occurred, literally on his doorstep. As a young lad he and his friends threw turf dust on the rails to watch the locomotives slip and looked into the wagons to see if it had been a good Dingle market.

Whilst I never saw any of the Irish narrow gauge railways in operation when they were working for a real living, I am also lucky enough to have met some eminent railway cognoscenti who did and who hardly stopped talking about them and their amazing experiences on visits for long weekends. Of course, my father was one of these, and so were Eric Russell, Ian Allan, Arthur Camwell and James Boyd. They, amongst many others, revelled in visits to see the dying embers of the remaining lines in the 1950s as, one by one, modernity killed them off. In the pre-digital age, they captured the final fair day and bank holiday specials in black & white, colour slide and even on cine film as they rushed from one line to another over weekend trips from England. Understandably, they were caught up in the magic of Ireland and the extraordinary railways they came

The County Donegal Railway Joint Committee survived until 1960, probably largely due to its use of diesel railcars to run as much of the traffic as possible, even towing wagons where practical, leaving the heavy freights and bank holiday passenger excursions to the geranium red tank engines. Here Railcar No. 10 (acquired from the Clogher Valley Railway) runs through the lonely Barnesmore Gap towing two wagons.

[Photo: P.B. Whitehouse]

Londonderry & Lough Swilly: These 4-8-4Ts were the largest narrow gauge steam engines in the British Isles and were built to provide the motive power on the Burtonport Extension. They weighed in at 53¾ tons. No. 6 is seen here at Londonderry Pennyburn engine shed.

[Photo: R.G. Jarvis]

across. Fortunately, they managed to collect some artefacts and records and begin research into the history and the reason for being of these railways and so many older images came to the surface. My father collected many of these images both for enjoying them for their own sake and using some in his Narrow Gauge Albums, now collectors items. Many of his friends freely gave their prints and 'PBW' was fortunate to acquire the collection of early and amazing photographs taken by prolific photographer Alfred W. Croughton. However, much of the picture reproduction in these books, whilst state of the art at the time, was by blocks made from prints using far fewer 'pixels' than is possible nowadays. This did not always enable the best reproduction and also, as such blocks were expensive, picture reproduction was somewhat limited and so several images never made the final cut into the books. Many have simply languished in the family files for over 50 years which seems a shame. So, here is a new book published with up to date technology which is able to show these images in a new and better format.

The choice of images is mine alone and some have, of course, been seen before. Originally, I intended to produce just one narrow gauge picture book for the narrow gauge railways of the whole of the British Isles, but I have been persuaded to produce more than one volume in order to show as many of the picture collection as practical. Inevitably, there will be a few mistakes as records are patchy in some cases. For example, my father kept no records, preferring to rush from one line to the next to capture as much as he could and also enjoy footplate rides and excellent Irish food and drink! On the other hand, Eric Russell kept meticulous records, even of exposures and certainly of dates and train times. Some prints have no information recorded on their reverse at all! Whilst, I have sought help in checking facts from histories and people who profess to know their subject, not everything will be perfect. Please enjoy the book in this light.

The text is almost wholly contemporary with the pictures. I thought this preferable to simply regurgitating histories or locomotive details. I have chosen a catholic selection of writings, ranging from descriptions of promotion and construction and spectacular accidents to train and footplate rides, written by eminent authors and also enthusiasts and, of course, some text from *Narrow Gauge Album* and *On the Narrow Gauge* has found its way into these pages, written by 'PBW' showing his enthusiasm for the subject.

Alfred W. Croughton was a prolific photographer and we are fortunate to have his many early photographs of narrow gauge railways all over the British Isles. He annotated his prints in purple ink and signed them all.

On their travels, the photographer adventurers met many lovely Irish people dedicated to their careers, offering footplate experiences and posing for the cameras; many of the pictures would not have been possible without this generosity. In memory of them all, some of the last words from the careful, meticulous and courteous Bernard Curran, the last secretary and manager of the County Donegal Railway Joint Committee, are worth quoting: *"When we cease operations on 1st January, 1960, one of the largest narrow gauge systems in Great Britain will be gone but, with the growth of the motor car and motor lorry, this was inevitable and we have carried on as long as was possible. At least I can say that we have provided a service to the people of Donegal and will continue to do so as a road organisation. Our history has been well recorded by the railway historians and the photographs of our line must now be legion – so we shall not be forgotten."*

But I will leave the very last word in this Introduction to 'PBW,' describing perhaps the compulsion to take just one more picture! In *Narrow Gauge Album*, 'PBW' admits to rather leaving the ladies to their own devices one evening as the temptation to chase the County Donegal train just a little further became too much: *'The last of these [County Donegal] excursions which I saw was in the summer of 1952. We passed the entrance to Ballyshannon station. As fortune would have it, there were signs of life and, what was more, the sight of steam on a fine day – so it seemed that a photograph was called for. We found out that a return excursion from Rossnowlagh to Strabane would be leaving later in the evening, so we pressed on to our hotel and, having seen to it that the ladies were comfortable, returned post haste to Ballyshannon, where we found the 2-6-4T Blanche sizzling quietly under the water tower…we followed her…by now, the evening shadows were lengthening, making photography difficult, but we resolved to follow her to Donegal… and then go on her way to Stranorlar. This we did, but it was not easy to turn our backs, for the train made a splendid sight in the gathering dusk. So we put behind us the knowledge that we were late already and followed her along the road, just that much further, and then made up our minds to see her on the bank. On then to the foot of the major climb, where we said farewell as the train made its way up alongside the dark mountain and away from the road, to disappear slowly with the smoke billowing away on the wind into the valley below.'*

Michael Whitehouse
Worcestershire, 2020

Narrow Gauge Railways in Ireland

[Extracted from the *Railway Magazine* 1904]

The industrial revival movement that is occupying such a large place in the minds of people of Ireland just now has brought into increasing prominence the important question of intercommunication in that country and, as a result, a number of schemes are already on foot for providing additional facilities for the free flow of traffic. It is opportune therefore to review the condition and prospects of a class of railway that in Ireland has had a large share in the opening up of the agricultural districts of the country.

In Ireland particular attention has been given to the development of railways of the narrow gauge type, and it is not surprising to find that these lines occupy a much more important position in the transit arrangements there than is the case in England. Thus the total length of 3ft narrow gauge railways open for traffic in Ireland at the end of 1902 amounted to 437 miles, or equal to about 13.5% of the total railway mileage, whilst in England and Wales the narrow gauge railway mileage amounted to only 132 miles, or hardly 1% of the total miles.

Scattered over Ireland, there are thirteen narrow gauge railway systems, worked as separate concerns. Eight companies, owning 298 miles of line, are situated in the northern portion of the island, and five companies, owning 139 miles, have established themselves in the south. The narrow gauge lines of Kerry and Donegal, two of the most congested districts, have been generously helped by grants from the Imperial Exchequer and, but for this assistance, it is probable that railway facilities would never have been established there.

The extensive adoption of narrow gauge railways in Ireland has been due to circumstances peculiar to that country. The districts through which these lines have been constructed are, for the most part, thinly populated, with few important towns on the route and possessing practically no industries that would be likely to create a large traffic. The promoters of railways in these outlying localities, therefore, considered that the volume of traffic to be expected would not have justified the building of costly broad gauge lines, and they decided to adopt in such cases, as an alternative, a less expensive system of communication, hence the large proportion of narrow gauge lines that have been constructed. In some cases the present narrow gauge lines were originally built on the broad gauge, but have since been converted, for the sake of economy in working.

As on the continent, many of these Irish narrow gauge lines run for a considerable portion of their length along the public highway, as the vehicular traffic on most of the roads is so light and of such a character that the local authorities have, as a rule, been willing to grant the necessary permission for the rails to be laid down and, whilst this arrangement has no doubt involved the negotiating of sharp curves and sometimes steep gradients, as well as reducing the speed limit, the saving in capital expenditure in the purchase of land has been a substantial set off against these disadvantages, and we, therefore, find the public roads being extensively used for this purpose. Further, the adoption of the 3ft gauge has been found to be more economical as regards the cost of rails, sleepers, and such like materials, and it has been stated by a competent authority that the cost of constructing a narrow gauge line is something like £1,400 per mile less than a broad gauge track under like circumstances. Then again, the prices of engines and rolling stock generally for the equipment of a narrow gauge railway would, of course, be proportionately less, and as respects the maintenance of the permanent way, sidings, and other works, there is little doubt that the advantages are on the side of the narrow gauge.

Turning to the question of the cost of working the two systems, as might be expected, a good deal of difference of opinion exists as to whether the narrow gauge lines are capable of being more economically worked than those of the broad gauge type. The matter was gone into at some length in 1888 at the Royal Commission on Irish Public Works, and most of the witnesses advocated the adoption of narrow gauge railways from an economical point of view. The arguments brought forward by Sir John Barton were interesting, and his large experience in the working of narrow gauge lines in the north of Ireland qualified him to speak with some authority on the subject. Sir John found that, in practice, the proportion of paying load to dead weight was much in favour of the 3ft. gauge railway.

At an early stage in the history of railway enterprise, the importance of affording every possible facility for the construction of railways in Ireland received the attention of the Imperial Parliament and, of the many enactments that have been sanctioned by the Legislature since 1860, by far the most important has been the **Tramways and Public Companies (Ireland) Act of 1883**, at any rate so far as the narrow gauge lines are concerned. The provisions of this Act were at the time considered somewhat novel and, as under it many of the class of railways that we are now dealing with have been built, it may not be amiss to attempt a brief *résumé* of its main features and glance at the results of its application.

The primary intention of the Act was to afford encouragement to those desirous of introducing railway communication into remote and outlying districts then without such facilities, and it provided amongst other things for the baronies through which the line was proposed to run, undertaking the financial responsibility for the scheme, perhaps to be afterwards shared by the Imperial Government. The promoters of a railway under the Act in the first place submitted the proposal to the Grand Jury of the county through which the line was to be made (the Grand Jury has since been superceded by the County Council as the authority), and the ratepayers might then oppose. The approval of the Grand Jury or County Council would throw on the rates of the county at large, or on the baronies through which the railway was proposed to be built, the charges not merely for interest on the cost of construction of the line, but the rates would be saddled as well with any deficit that might occur in connection with the working, and further, if the line was abandoned by the promoters, the responsibility for operating it was also placed on the contributing baronies. The project having passed the Grand Jury required the sanction of the Privy Council and, if opposition was still maintained at that stage, the scheme required to be confirmed by an Act of Parliament. The confirmation by Parliament carried with it

an obligation to repay the Grand Jury either interest on the capital expenditure to the extent of 2% or half the difference between the net receipts and the total guaranteed interest, whichever might be the smaller.

While in many respects the Act of 1883 was a great advancement on previous measures in connection with the extension of local railways in the poorer districts of Ireland, on the whole it has not operated satisfactorily and, to a large extent, it has failed in accomplishing the object for which it was intended. It is now 13 years since the last Order in Council was issued authorising the construction of a narrow gauge line on a baronial security, and it is unlikely that the provisions of the Act will be further availed of.

The reasons for the comparative failure of the measure were fully dwelt on by the various witnesses at the Royal Commission on Irish Public Works previously referred to. It was shown that the districts most in need of relief in the way of railway facilities, to enable the people to obtain an outlet for their produce and connect them with the outside world, were poor and mountainous, where the rates and taxes pressed heavily on the inhabitants and the people therefore found themselves unable to bear an additional tax for railways or tramways. Again, it was contended that the financial arrangements of the Act did not fully utilise the credit of the State and the country, the guarantee was surrounded with contingencies that cautious capitalists did not like, and the result was that, while the Treasury could easily raise money at 3%, the combined guarantee afforded by the Act was found not to tempt capitalists even at 5%.

But the chief defect, and the one that appealed most strongly to the ratepayers in the guaranteeing area, was that the financial arrangements were not calculated to ensure economy in constructing the line or enterprise in working it. The capital was guaranteed on the security of the baronies at the high rate of 5% and, when this was absolutely secured to the shareholders, whether the undertaking was successful or not, there was but little inducement to economise and work the line at a profit.

Further the working of these railways as separate concerns has been found to be very expensive, and the results are certainly not encouraging. If these lines had been built as broad gauge railways it may be assumed that the loss in working would however have been very much greater.

Thus for the last available year, 1901-02, the ratepayers in the baronies through which six of the railways run (Cavan & Leitrim, Clare, Clogher Valley, Cork & Muskerry, Schull & Skibbereen and Tralee & Dingle) had to pay in respect of the interest on the capital outlay and the deficit in working the lines a sum of no less than £25,149, while the loss to the Treasury for the same period was £14,485, making a total loss on these railways of £39,634 for the 12 months. The extra tax on the ratepayers in the contributing areas, represented by the sum of £25,149, averaged about 4½d in the £. This is surely a high price to pay for the privilege of having a railway in one's district, and the Irish farmers have, therefore, strenuously opposed the introduction of any more of these baronial guaranteed lines.

In addition to the six companies owning the 216 miles previously referred to, there are seven other narrow gauge railways which own 221 miles of railway. The most successful of these is the Londonderry and Lough Swilly Railway (49 miles), whose working expenses are extremely low and whose shareholders have received for a number of years a dividend of 7% per annum on the ordinary stock. The Donegal Railway (90 miles) has been largely helped from the Imperial Treasury in connection with the construction of lines in the congested district of County Donegal, and a dividend of 4.5% per annum is paid. The Belfast & Northern Counties Railway, recently purchased by the Midland Railway of England, works 48 miles of narrow gauge mileage, and has hitherto paid a dividend of 5%. The Castlederg and Victoria Bridge Tramway, 7 miles long, pays 3% per annum.

The Ballycastle Railway, the Cork, Blackrock and Passage Railway and the Bessbrook Tramway have not yet been able to pay anything to the holders of the ordinary shares.

From these figures it will be seen that out of 13 companies but four have been able to pay, out of revenue, any dividend on the ordinary shares. Excluding the four dividend paying companies, the mileage of the remaining narrow gauge lines is 243 miles, the gross earnings of them for the year 1902 being £88,592, and the expenditure £88,027, representing a net gain in working of only £565. In other words the expenditure works out about 99% of the gross receipts. If the future promises no better result than this, the prospect of Ireland's development by means of narrow gauge railways is poor indeed. It is, however, right to observe that the industrial outlook in Ireland is at present encouraging. The great interest that is being taken in technical education, and the sympathetic attitude of the agricultural classes toward the new Land Bill, as well as the movement having for its object the revival of the decaying industries of the country, are, we think indications of better times and the increasing prosperity will no doubt have a reflex influence on the condition of these railways.

In taking leave of this subject it must be remembered that the great weakness in the financial position of these little lines is the heavy expense of working them as separate concerns, necessitating a complete administrative staff for each company, with the usual complement of directors. The remedy would appear to lie in the direction of the amalgamation of these small non paying concerns on terms to be arranged, and the establishment of a central bureau charged with their administration, and as the total capital invested in these undertakings does not exceed £1,500,000, the difficulties would not appear to be insurmountable. An object lesson of this is afforded in Belgium, where the circumstances are not much dissimilar. In that country, the control of these local railways is vested in the *Societe Nationale de Chemins de Fer Vicinaux*, which was formed in 1885, during a time of agricultural depression, with the object of promoting inexpensive narrow gauge railways through the outlying districts, and a central administration has the oversight of these lines. The financial results of this model of organisation have proved, on the whole, satisfactory and, instead of the railways being a burden on the ratepayers and the Government, as is the case in Ireland, the working profit has enabled a dividend to be paid to the shareholders.

We can see nothing to prevent something of the kind being attempted in Ireland. In any case, the matter is one that deserves consideration of the directors involved.

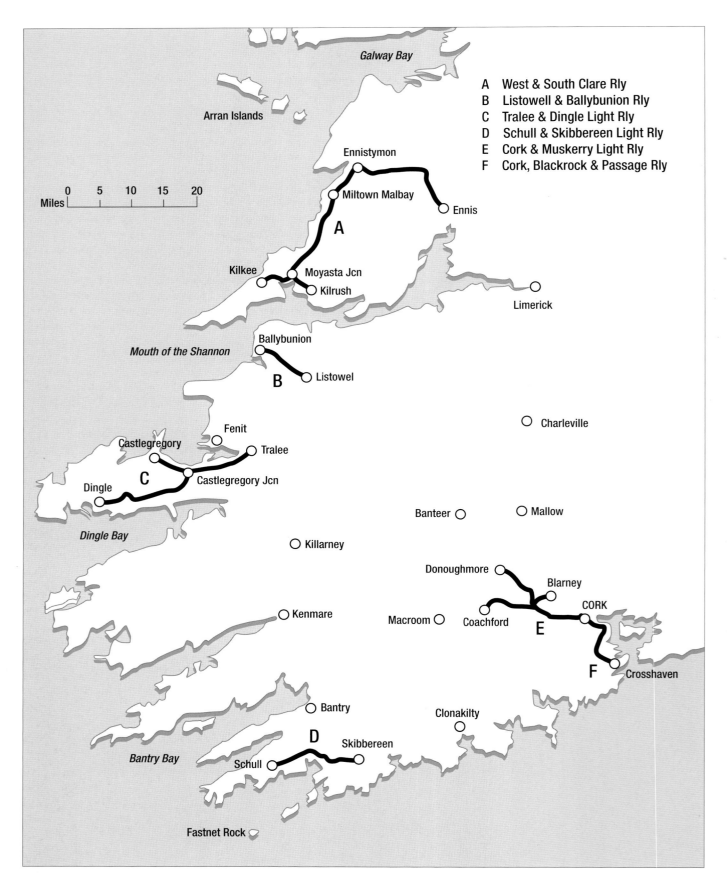

Galway Bay

Arran Islands

A West & South Clare Rly
B Listowell & Ballybunion Rly
C Tralee & Dingle Light Rly
D Schull & Skibbereen Light Rly
E Cork & Muskerry Light Rly
F Cork, Blackrock & Passage Rly

Ennistymon

Miltown Malbay

Ennis

Miles
0 5 10 15 20

Kilkee

Moyasta Jcn

Kilrush

A

Limerick

Ballybunion

Mouth of the Shannon

Listowel

B

Charleville

Fenit

Castlegregory

Tralee

Dingle

Castlegregory Jcn

C

Banteer

Mallow

Killarney

Dingle Bay

Kenmare

Donoughmore

Blarney

CORK

Macroom

Coachford

E

F

Crosshaven

Bantry

Clonakilty

D

Skibbereen

Bantry Bay

Schull

Fastnet Rock

Narrow Gauge
in the Republic
of Ireland

RAIL-VIADUCT. BALLYDEHOB .Co. CORK. 10264. W.L.

Three foot gauge Peckett & Sons, *Gabriel*, built in 1906, poses for a publicity picture on the 12 arched Ballydehob viaduct carrying the Schull & Skibbereen Railway over an inlet in Roaringwater Bay estuary, County Cork, around 1908. The locomotive is wearing a spark arrestor on its chimney and hauling carriages No's 5 and 7, passenger brake van (probably No. 54) and covered wagons No's 31, 32 and 38. The tramway was 15.5 miles long and, apart from this significant viaduct, ran mainly along the roadside from the market town of Skibbereen, connecting with the 5ft 3in. branch to Baltimore, to the fishing village of Schull on the waters of the Bay. [Photo: National Library, Dublin]

The Tram

J.I.C. Boyd

[The Schull & Skibbereen]

One could hardly blame the English visitor for his sense of relief. After all, he had a rough night on the mail boat and it had been the devil of a way across Dublin to the station at Kingsbridge. And then the train had messed about at some place, Limerick Junction they said, where they went forward and then back, and then forward again, in a most distracting and annoying way. When Cork had at last been reached, he had had to take a cab some distance through the streets and over the River Lee to the small station at Albert Quay. Then for another two hours the train had wrestled with

the hills as the country grew more lush – Bantry, Drimoleague (more shunting) and at last Skibbereen, the beginning of the last stage of this endless journey to Schull. His temper frayed, as well it might; these locals ran their railways with such light hearted off-handedness, polite yes, but easy going almost to the point of downright slackness. Anyway, he had changed trains at last and now he sat, with such relief as was justified, whilst a little bright green engine with a large cowcatcher and a drooping lamp under its chimney suddenly nudged the end of the train. He almost fell into the lap of his neighbour, an

No. 4, *Erin*, a 4-4-0T built by Naysmith Wilson & Co. in 1888, stands by the water tank and in front of the turntable at Schull with the driver 'Curly' Hegarty posing on the running board. The line was built with Government assistance under the terms of the Tramways Act, 1883, but the only deference to that on this locomotive was its cowcatcher. No. 4 was the first locomotive in Ireland to have a Belpaire firebox and the fitting of Walschaerts valve gear was also an exceptional feature at that time.

Although the formal name for the Schull & Skibbereen was The West Carberry Tramways and Light Railway Company Ltd, it quickly became known as 'The Sick & Sore Railway' or 'The Tram'. Construction was begun in 1885 and soon proved to be substandard. The Inspector of Railways refused to allow the line to be opened for public service in August 1886. Following some remedial work and a subsequent inspection, the line opened in September with a restricted speed limit of only 15mph. In October the service had to be suspended for 10 days owing to problems with both the track and the locomotives. Services had to again be suspended in April 1887, with local ratepayers having to subsidise the company. The Inspector of Railways gave a highly critical report of the line's standards of operation. Here we see one of three tram locomotives built by Dick, Kerr of Kilmarnock in 1886 for the opening of the line, No. 2 once named *Ida*, the last survivor of the trio, stands at Skibbereen on 29th May, 1924, the last year of the line's independence. No. 2, a well tank 0-4-0 tramway engine, cased in to meet Board of Trade requirements, was scrapped in 1926, a year after the Great Southern Railway took the line over. The other two tram locomotives were called *Marion* and *Ilen*.
[Photo: A.W. Croughton]

Dick, Kerr also supplied the original four wheeled carriages for the tramway. First class No. 1 and a third class carriage stand in Schull station at the end of a mixed train with two local lads posing on the back balcony in early Great Southern Railway days.

old peasant woman sitting alongside. The coach was small, with balconies at each end, and the people sat face to face and knee to knee as they did on the bottom deck of the buses back in London. On their knees they carried baskets and boxes of chickens whilst, on the floor, two small piglets squeaked with fear.

A snatch of the couplings and they were off, but no sooner had they started than they shuddered to a standstill again. Goodness, surely not another hold up? No, here they were moving backwards again – perhaps they had forgotten to pick up something – no, they were on another line. Now the train was stopping again; it had stopped. When would this madness cease? This was Limerick Junction all over again. He sensed that feeling of annoyance coming over him once more. With another jerk and a shriek from a piglet as the motion threw it off balance, they drew forward again…no surely not, but yes, out of a small gate onto and across a road…no protecting gates to stop anything running into the train, but then there was only a donkey cart some distance away.

Now the engine really had got going. The little coach plunged and jostled along, and his spirits rose. The engine whistled – a tuneful sound. He almost felt like whistling. Now and then bushes and trees wiped along the outside of the coach where he was sitting and he instinctively leant forward. The others in the little carriage were beginning already to nod but a cooling breeze swept from one open end door to the other and fanned him gently. Of course, it was hardly a railway train as he had imagined it; it ran alongside the road like a tramcar, and now and then overtook horses and donkeys attached to small carts. Once a horse and cart passed them! He liked that. Everyone seemed to know everybody else and passers by waved to the train as if it too was a personal friend. The guard came down the coach and asked for his ticket, passing from one bumping carriage to another by a small gate in the end railing of the balcony.

Once or twice the little train stopped beside the road to pick up and set down people. On another occasion it left the road and ran across rocky moorland and halted beneath an old wooden water tank. At times the going was very fast and the coach heaved and rolled, at others the train could hardly surmount several of the steep hillocks which followed each bend. Then the sea came in sight, and what a wonderful view it

Overleaf: A second picture of *Erin*, this time by the turntable at Skibbereen on 29th May, 1924. The locomotive is now also sporting a spark arrestor on its chimney. Skibbereen was the base for the locomotives and carriages and also had a small repair shop.   [Photo: A.W. Croughton]

Peckett & Co. of Bristol built two 4-4-0Ts to complete the replacement of the original tram engines. The first of these was 1906 built *Gabriel*, works No. 1085 seen here at Schull station in 1933. Three years later, the locomotive was scrapped when its boiler failed. [Photo: A.W. Croughton]

was right across Roaringwater Bay, with Clear Island away in the mist, the first land sighted by travellers from the Americas. All round the gorse was in bloom, a fiery yellow, and the train lifted the dust on the rough road alongside to swirl it in clouds behind. There was quite a busy station at Ballydehob with a proper platform, and then they crossed a long stone viaduct and began to climb the opposing hill with weary belching from the engine. They tried hard but the train must have been too heavy and they stuck. What would happen next? This sort of thing was not allowed to happen in England. Some men came running from the fields nearby and put their shoulders to the corners of the carriages. Yes, they were moving…at last they had done it…the pushers dropped off one by one, and stood panting on the rails. Onwards went the little train, away from the road now and through gorse, heather and rocky bluffs, so back to the road again, twisting and turning as it went, through a treeless upland so different from anywhere else he had been. They stopped to pick up some children where there was a notice in the fence: 'Woodlands' it said. And there wasn't a single tree in sight – well, if that wasn't Ireland for you!

With so much running beside the road he would hardly have noticed that they had suddenly left it, save that the roar of the rock walls as they plunged down a cutting seemed very loud through the open doors. There was a squeal from the floor, not from the piglet this time, but the brake blocks gripping the spinning wheels. A smell of hot iron bit into the compartment and, through the window, he saw the little engine swing suddenly round a sharp bend over a stream. Looking back he could see how steeply they had dropped. They must be near Schull now. Yes, here was the road again and they had crossed it. He had a momentary glimpse of flying hens and geese, and the train drew up, still in the hot aroma of burning metal. Bags, baggage, piglets; the people rose and, before he had collected all his gear, the platform was almost deserted. A small barefoot boy, raggedly dressed, offered to carry his things. Almost without knowing, he consented. Out on the platform a woman was unconcernedly mangling the newly washed clothes and, as she worked, a little girl came struggling along with a tin bath of hot water, delivered from a little pipe beneath the engine's steps. He had hardly noticed it, but the tedium of the last 24 hours had left him, and he was obliged to admit that he wished he could have journeyed farther by the West Carbury tram.

No. 3, *Kent*, the second 4-4-0T from Peckett & Sons, works No. 1356, built slightly later in 1914, seen here at Skibbereen on 29th May, 1924. Originally the locomotive was named *Conciliation*, but it was renamed after Thomas Kent, the Irish nationalist, who was executed by the British at Cork goal in the aftermath of the 1916 Easter Rising. No. 3 was similar to *Gabriel* but slightly shorter and with a smaller boiler. She was scrapped in 1953. [Photo: A.W. Croughton]

Schull & Skibbereen train at Hollyhill on 1st July, 1938. 'Curly' Hegarty drives engine No. 4 *Erin* passing a horse and cart on the road. There were usually two return trains daily, with an extra on Schull and Ballydehob cattle fair days. The journey took an hour and a half. The railway was run on a shoestring budget and never made any money. The locals learned that for speed and punctuality they were probably better off with road transport and this, eventually, brought about closure on 27th January, 1947. [Photo: H.C. Casserley]

Gabriel **stands in Schull station with a two coach passenger train whilst the train crew and station staff all pose for the photographer.**
[Photo: A.W. Croughton]

Skibbereen engine shed on 4th September, 1954. [Photo: K. C. Cooper]

Schull engine shed on 4th August, 1953. [Photo: K.C. Cooper]

Built by Thomas Green & Sons in 1893, works No. 200 6S, originally named *The Muskerry*, an 0-4-4T transferred from the Cork & Muskerry Tramway in 1938, stands on the turntable at Schull. She was reputed to have done little work subsequently and was scrapped in 1953.

Ivo Peters recalls: *"During the post war coal crisis, the railway was 'temporarily closed' in December 1946, never to re-open. Sadly I never saw the line in action, but on one of my visits to Ireland in 1950, I had an amazing piece of good luck. On going to Skibbereen on 3rd July, I found, to my delight, one of the Schull & Skibbereen engines in steam and in the process of pulling out the narrow gauge stock for Mr Cyril Fry, an eminent Irish railway enthusiast."* So, here we see No. 6S pulling Peckett 4-4-0T *Kent* out of the engine shed for photography.
[Photo: Ivo Peters]

Cyril Fry is seen here at Skibbereen measuring up a balconied bogie carriage built in 1897 by the Gloucester Railway Carriage & Wagon Co. No. 6S stands with steam feathering from its safety valve having performed the shunt moves to enable the measuring to take place. 3rd July, 1950. Apparently, Cyril Fry wanted a private steaming and was not amused by Ivo Peters' appearance and told him to go away! [Photo: Ivo Peters]

On 3rd July, 1950, over three years after the railway had closed, 0-4-4T No. 6S was in steam in Skibbereen yard! She became stuck on these points. Apparently during her sojourn on the line, she had never previously had to negotiate this particular set of points and its radius proved too tight for her. Manual effort with crowbars set things to rights. [Photo: Ivo Peters]

04-4-T No. 6S out of use besides Skibbereen engine shed in 1950. [Photo: P.B. Whitehouse]

The derelict Woodlands halt on 4th August, 1953. Not a tree in sight! [Photo: K.C. Cooper]

4-4-0T No. 4, *Blarney* (the second locomotive of that name), built by Hunslet, Works No. 1200, construction beginning in 1914 but not delivered until 1919 due to the war. Locomotive cut up in 1927 after a short life. Seen here at Cork (Western Road) on 28th May, 1924. [Photo: A.W. Croughton]

Chapter Two

The Cork and Muskerry Light Railway
By J.P. O'Keefe
[adapted from the Railway Magazine 1898]

On 25th April, 1884, the promoters of the Cork and Muskerry Light Railway presented a memorial to the Lord Lieutenant of Ireland, praying for an Order in Council to authorise the construction and laying down of a light railway between Cork and Coachford, 15.5 miles; and also a branch therefrom to Blarney, 2.5 miles. The Corporation of Cork and the Grand Jury of the County of Cork approved of the undertaking; notwithstanding this, there were several petitions lodged against the confirmation of the presentment made by the Grand Jury at the previous March Assizes. From that date to the opening of the line in 1887 the promoters had to face strong opposition. In June, 1886, they succeeded in getting the Order in Council of the Lord Lieutenant confirmed. It is not easy at the present day to account for such persistent opposition as was carried to the very threshold of the Confirmation Act by most of the farmers in the district through which it was proposed to run the railway, and by some of the citizens of Cork, who had little to lose but much to gain,

4-4-0T No. 7, formerly named *Peake* and ordered from Brush Electrical Engineering Co. (the successors to the Falcon Works) in 1887, heads the 12.05 pm Cork (Western Road) to Donoughamore via Blarney on a misty 7th October, 1933. The locomotive was scrapped two years later.

[Photo: A.W. Croughton]

0-4-4T No. 6, *Muskerry* Class 'ENI' built by Thomas Green at Cork (Western Road) on 28th May, 1924. [Photo: A.W. Croughton]

Cork Station in 1924 with 4-4-0T No. 8 *Dripsey* built by Brush Electrical Engineering Co. (the successors to Falcon Works) in 1904, Works No. 307. This was the last locomotive built for the line.

as after events have proved. Armed with the Act of Parliament, and the authorised capital of the Company - £75,000, in 15,000 shares of £5 each – having been fully subscribed, the Directors who deserve well of the public for the energetic manner in which they pushed forward the project, were not slow in building the line from Cork to Blarney, 8.75 miles, through a most picturesque and richly-wooded valley. The first passenger train was despatched from Cork on the morning of 8th August, 1887. In the following March, the main line to Coachford, which passes through a rich and fertile agricultural district, was completed. The directors and the public, seeing the great advantage to agriculturalists in the surrounding districts by the marked success of this line, applied for and obtained an Order in Council authorising the construction of an extension from St. Anns to Donoughmore, 8.5 miles, with a capital of £35,000, which was opened for traffic in May, 1893, making a total mileage on the Company's system of 27 miles, which has opened up a large tract of country, both as a source of industrial supply and as a means of enjoyment for thousands of pleasure seekers.

The Cork terminus is situated on the Western Road, and consists of a spacious and well constructed station, providing every convenience for the administrative departments and the general business of the company. The rolling stock is of the most improved type; at the opening of the line it consisted of only three engines, 22 four ton wagons, four third class and two composite first and third class carriages and two guard's vans. At present there are seven engines, four wheeled coupled (five with leading and two with trailing bogies), one constructed by Kitson & Co. Leeds, two by Green and Sons, Leeds and four at the Falcon Engine Works, Loughborough; 66 six ton wagons, 21 carriages and six guard's vans to work the traffic. The passenger coaches, which are admirably suited for the accommodation of passengers, are mounted on two four wheel bogies and fitted with vacuum brakes; they are 30ft long and can seat 40 passengers each. The wagons and carriages were supplied by the Falcon Engine Works, Loughborough, the Metropolitan Railway Carriage and Wagon Company, Birmingham, the Oldbury Railway Carriage and Wagon Company, Limited, and Messrs. Craven Brothers, Sheffield; with this increase to the rolling stock the carriages are sometimes found inadequate to the demand during the tourist season, nor can it be said that there is a sufficient supply of wagons to cope with the heavy traffic on fair days.

This has been a most successful line and has proved a boon to the farmer, which he now readily admits. It has been a saving of several pounds annually to him; instead of the long journeys to Cork in wet and inclement weather prior to the opening of the railway, he can now come to town in a comfortable carriage, do his business, and get home again in a few hours; speak to him of his former opposition, he will hang down his head and blush – it is not an easy matter to paint an Irish farmer's face crimson.

The task of providing the railway was undertaken by the

4-4-0T No. 2 heads a train running through the streets of Cork under the wires of the electric tram track on 10th June, 1932. Amazingly the steam tramway outlived the electric one by three years and a few carriages still exist built into local homes. [Photo: H.C. Casserley]

promoters and carried out in a most successful manner to their mutual benefit. The farmer's produce is brought to market for a few shillings per ton, the feeding stuffs for his cattle are carried out at a like low rate, his children can travel to school at a cheap fare, the old jog of man and horse by night along the high road is given up. The stage house, with its aired beer and bread is abandoned, and the old clay pipe gives place to a well shaped meerschaum. The cost of maintaining the county roads in the vicinity of the railway has been considerably reduced. One who had not watched the gradual progress of this line would be surprised at the vast change it has made in the districts through which it passes – dull and monotonous country districts have become a scene of activity and business; hotels, refreshment saloons, cafes and public houses have increased along the line, and several creameries have been built, one of which got first prize for its butter at a recent exhibition held in London. Altogether 30,225 gallons of milk passed over the line during the month of March, 1898, although not one of the best months for this class of traffic. The milk is taken to the creamery in the morning, manufactured into butter, packed in neat, clean, white deal boxes and despatched by an evening train for Cork and arrives in England next morning pure Irish, fresh and wholesome and cheap; at this the farmer cannot grumble, the only fault is there are not more light railways in Ireland.

Dripsey station, on the main line, 12 miles from Cork,

beautifully situated on the Valley of the Lee, is much frequented by the angler, artist and tourist. Coachford is a small village charmingly situated on the northern bank of the River Lee. It is rapidly increasing in importance in consequence of the facilities of communication afforded by the railway and the large cattle, sheep and pig fairs held there monthly. The fairs held at Donoughmore are also large and well attended. Blarney is the most attractive, and perhaps the most interesting, station on this railway. Its far famed castle and beautiful groves are widely known and visited by many tourists. The castle was built about the middle of the fifteenth century. Its massive donjon tower is 120ft high, and can be ascended by a spiral stone staircase of 188 steps. The celebrated Blarney stone is placed on the western angle about 20ft from the top; to kiss it, the bold must be suspended by the heels over the battlements at the risk of breaking his neck! When looking back over the first few years after the opening of this railway, with only six carriages and three engines to work the enormous passenger traffic, I cannot help asking how it was done?

It is owing to the skill of the General Manager, Mr J.B. Wilson, whose many years of railway experience in the Dublin and Meath and Navan and Kingscourt Railways, and also the Dublin and Lucan Steam Tramway, well befitted him for such an undertaking. The Company shows very satisfactory progress from a commercial point of view. The £5 shares, which formerly stood at par, are now worth £8, with prospects

Inspecting the damage! A runaway steam roller hit the 7.45 am train from Donoughmore to Cork at Inchigoggin on 6th September, 1927 on the Carrigrohane Road. Whose fault the accident was has never been resolved. The locomotive driver claimed he blew his whistle when within 40 yards of the steam roller and again when nearer to it but, on the other hand, the roller driver claimed that he signalled the train to stop. The story that the two were having a race took a long time to live down!

of further advancement, the last report disclosing a steady increase of traffic over the returns of the previous half years. At the first meeting of the Directors and shareholders, held on 21st February, 1888, after the opening of the Blarney line, the Chairman, R. Barter Esq. said: "*There are some points which, in looking into a little, will, I think, prove both interesting and gratifying to you. In the first place, our gross receipts on the Blarney section from passenger traffic alone are nearly £2,000 for 20 weeks working. This creditable return would have been a good deal more had we sufficient rolling stock.*" At the half yearly meeting, held on 22nd February, 1898, the Chairman, referring to the continual increase in traffic, said: "*The New Tramway Company had met them very harmoniously, and were making their gauge exactly to suit that of the Muskerry Railway. They had been in communication with the Chairman of the Cork and Passage Railway Company, who met them in a very friendly spirit, so that they (the Muskerry Company) would be able to run a coach through from Coachford to Crosshaven (40 miles). That was something that would open the eyes of those who sneered originally at the Muskerry line.*"

The railway runs for 3.75 miles on the public road, 2.5 miles of which is on a raised siding 9in high. The portion within the borough's boundary is on a level with the road. The sleepers are set on a concrete bed, the space between the rails (three foot) and a foot outside is paved with granite sets, therefore the vehicular traffic is not in the slightest degree impeded.

Victoria is a suburban station. Carrigrohane, 3.5 miles from Cork, where the line winds its way at the base of a massive limestone rock, is the next. The natural grandeur of this spot has attracted many tourists, and is a favourite resort of the citizens of Cork. At Leemount, the train goes off the public road, and the speed is increased to 25mph. The scenery along the lovely valley of the River Shournagh to Healy's Bridge is most charming. St. Anns, where the Donoughmore line branches off, is the next station to Blarney. It is remarkable for its first class passenger traffic. This is principally due to the widely known and highly appreciated health resort, St. Anns Hill Hydropathic Establishment, which is beautifully situated on rising ground within a few minutes walk of the station. The entire journey from Cork to Blarney, making allowance for seven stops and reduced speed on the public road, is performed in 37 minutes. The first class return fare from Cork to Blarney on week days is only 1/2d, third class 10d; on Sundays one shilling first and ninepence third. On weekdays there are six trains to and from Blarney, five from Coachford, and three from Donoughmore. On Sundays the trains run to Blarney every two hours from 10am to 8pm; there are only two both ways between Cork and Coachford and Cork and Donoughmore. The trains are worked on the staff and ticket system in conjunction with the telephone, which is connected with the different sections along the line.

The extraordinary success of this undertaking affords a striking example of the numerous advantages conferred on the public, and proves forcibly that the extension of light railways in Ireland would go far to improve the social and financial position of the tenant farmer and establish a spirit of competition among them hitherto unknown in the remote districts to the Irish agriculturalist. I hope the time has come when every person interested in the welfare and prosperity of the country will forget any mistakes that might have been made in the past, and work together as one united body for its future development. The construction and successful working of light railways form the foremost effort of obtaining such a desirable end.

Chapter Three

Narrow Gauge Enterprise
By Pat Whitehouse
(The Cork, Blackrock & Passage Railway)
Extracted from Narrow Gauge Album

How often an old timetable can tell a story or complete a picture in the mind's eye! Through the kindness of a friend, I had the chance to pore over a time and fare table of the old Cork, Blackrock & Passage Railway, dated Tuesday 1st June, 1909, a year when the railway was at the peak of its narrow gauge career (for 50 years it was broad gauge line before it was narrowed to 3ft gauge after the construction of the Crosshaven Extension in 1900). The old booklet was full of interest. As with many timetables of that day, most of the contents comprised advertisements, mainly extolling the virtues of local shops, restaurants and hotels, but several pages were devoted to special fares and facilities offered

by the Railway Company. These included a trip on the River Lee and around Cork Harbour, including lunch, for 3/6d. (the Company owned its own steamships), and a Grand Circular Tour of Cork Harbour in conjunction with the broad gauge Great Southern & Western Railway. Through return excursion tickets were available in conjunction with the neighbouring railway companies and workmens' tickets were issued at all stations on the Cork, Blackrock & Passage Railway's line and also on the Company's steamships. In addition to those tickets, there were season tickets, childrens' tickets (under 18 years of age), nine day's tickets, family tickets (in bundles of not less than 12 at a reduction of 10%) and, finally, combined railway

Double tracked narrow gauge: A Cork to Passage mixed train on the only main line section of narrow gauge double track in the British Isles built to cater for the busy Cork commuter traffic. The train is hauled by one of the railway's four 2-4-2Ts. [Photo: Rex Murphy]

Journey's end: Crosshaven station which received 11 daily trains from Cork. The station platform boasts peep show, chocolate, weighing and print your name machines ubiquitous to railway stations all over the British Isles at the time. A 2-4-2T is in the headshunt, partly shielded by the station building, whilst running round its train.
[Photo: National Library, Dublin]

RAILWAY STATION. CROSSHAVEN. 8853. W.L.

Express tank engine: Neilson Reid 2-4-2T of 1900 No. 4 at Cork Albert Street station on 28th May, 1924. [Photo: A.W. Coughton]

The first train on the Crosshaven Extension in 1904. The 2-4-2T is bedecked with flags carried on its smokebox.

and hotel tickets in conjunction with the Crosshaven Hotel. The offer here was for bed & breakfast for one week, six return tickets, all first class, between Cork and Crosshaven at a cost of only 45/-. Perhaps the most unique advertisement was a whole page offering a first class free pass between Cork and any station of the railway at any time, to the owner or one member of the family of any new house of suitable character, built adjacent to any station on the line. Depending on the value of the house, this pass could be available for three or five years.

Turning to the actual timetable pages, there were 11 trains between Cork and Crosshaven every day, with 13 trains daily to Monkstown on weekdays, and 10 and 11 respectively on Sundays only. This was a really fine service for an Irish narrow gauge railway and reveals the weight of suburban and tourist passenger traffic at that time. (Unfortunately, the latter traffic was at its peak for only four months out of the 12). Of particular interest was a daily express in each direction, completing the 16 mile journey in 35 minutes, no mean feat for a narrow gauge line when the numerous slacks are taken into consideration. On summer Sundays the trains ran at half hour intervals during afternoons. The line was double between Cork and Blackrock and this was the only example of a double track main line on any narrow gauge railway in the British Isles. It was singled by the Great Southern Railways in 1927 as a desperate measure of economy.

As the total number of locomotives was only four, there was little margin left for emergencies and the Neilson Reid 2-4-2 outside cylinder tanks gave excellent service. These engines had the largest driving wheel of any Irish narrow gauge locomotive

and were painted black with vermillion and white lining. The carriage stock was composed entirely of bogie coaches, some of which were arranged in the form of saloons. One of these coaches was generally marshalled at the rear of each train and their seats eagerly sought by the tourist passengers. The stations and permanent way were probably the best maintained of any narrow gauge line in Ireland.

In spite of this enterprising timetable, the fortunes of the railway were on the decline, for the Crosshaven Extension had proved costly to construct and the Company's existence soon became so precarious that it was only just able to meet the interest on the heavy issue of Debenture stock of 1901. The Tramway, which from 1901 onwards had been running to Blackrock Village, added considerably to the Company's financial worries and practically wiped out the suburban traffic. Nevertheless, the railway just managed to outlive the trams by a year.

The end came in 1932 when the Great Southern Railways terminated all services, first from Monkstown to Crosshaven on 31st May and the remainder of the line on 10th September. The route of the railway was four miles longer than the road journey and the buses and cars had taken all the traffic from the line; this, coupled with the fact that the once prosperous days of the Passage dockyards were now only a memory, sealed its fate.

Few relics now remain of this once popular transport system, although the locomotives and many wagons were transferred to the Cavan & Leitrim Section of the GSR (now Coras Iompair Eireann).

After the 'Troubles': A train headed by one of the four 2-4-2Ts standing posed over Rochestown bridge while it was under repair by railway troops of the Irish army after being blown up by Republicans in 1922.

Chapter Four

Once Daily and Once Monthly
J.I.C. Boyd
[West Clare and Tralee & Dingle]

Having travelled over the Cavan & Leitrim section of the C.I.E, we were naturally anxious to cover the remaining narrow gauge lines still open for traffic in Eire. There were, by 1949, only two such systems open, being the former West and South Clare lines and the Tralee & Dingle. So, we travelled overnight from Holyhead, eventually leaving Westland Row at 8.40am on the combined Galway and Sligo train which divides at Mullingar. The run across to Athenry on the former Midland & Great Western system behind one of the 2-6-0 locomotives erected from parts made at Woolwich Arsenal, the most powerful type then on the former Great Southern system, was without note, there being ample stops at Mullingar, Athlone and stations beyond to Athenry, the area of the great bog stretching as far as eye

RAIL-STATION·KILRUSH·6335·W·L·

Kilrush, one of the two eastern termini of the West Clare section, a market town *'that will not detain the tourist long'* [H. Fayle] on the River Shannon estuary, with a train and the station staff posed in the early years of the West Clare Railway for the photographer whilst he exposes his glass plate negative. The mixed train of six wheeler carriages and a single cattle van is headed by No. 4 *Besborough*, one of the four Bagnall 0-6-0 side tank engines built in 1887 for the opening of the line, named after the Earl of Besborough, a local magnate. These four locomotives were made to Bagnall's own design and dealt with all the traffic until 1892; they then became too small for the traffic and were replaced around the turn of the century, with No. 4 being the first to be withdrawn in 1901. [Photo: National Library, Dublin]

Kilkee station, serving a seaside resort and one of the best known 'watering places' in Ireland, being the other eastern termini. The town clusters round a protected bay with an excellent strand and a well known golf course and famous for its very bracing air. All the line's carriages were six wheelers; the one in the near part of the picture being a first class example. [Photo: National Library, Dublin]

Class 'IN1', No. 5C, *Slieve Callan*, an 0-6-2T built by Dubs in 1892 and the first of the replacement locomotives for the original Bagnalls. No. 5C still exists and, after being plinthed for many years at Ennis, has been returned to working order being based at the preservation scheme at Moyasta Junction. Here No. 5C sports a lined out livery specially applied for filming *A Minute's Wait*. [Photo: Cork Examiner]

Kilrush, an outside framed 4-6-0T, introduced by W.J. Carter to the design of William Barrington, the consulting engineer to the West Clare Railway, as new No. 1 and built by Hunslet in 1912, works No. 1098, designated Class 'BN3'. No. 1 stands at Ennis on 31st May, 1924 lined out in WCR livery. [Photo: A. W. Croughton]

can see to north and south of the train, and differing little in character as we went west. At Athenry, we changed into the daily train from Sligo to Limerick and, in an hour, we were in Ennis along a more rocky coastal belt, where we had a wait of three hours.

Outside the carriage repair shops were the saloons used for tourist traffic during the summer. They were now stored, though the first class vehicle is now the yard forman's office. The remainder of the stock is of the six compartment type, built by Bristol Carriage and Wagon for the opening of the line in 1887. It is lit from a carbide gas plant in the guard's van. Most of it is now in C.I.E green with the 'Flying Snail' totem. It should be remarked that all the Clare stock runs on six wheels and that wheelbases are quite long. There are no sharp curves on this line, however. There are one or two bogie vans transferred from the Dingle line.

Engine No. 5 was in steam in the yard (0-6-2T Dubs of 1892) whilst No. 10 was on shed having new brake blocks fitted. This engine is peculiar in having the valve gear arranged forward of the leading driving axle between the frames. The reversing links are hung with their centres of circle on the eccentric instead of more conventionally with their centre taken from the valve rod pin. The drive is through rocker arms onto the valve chests outside the frame.

The repair shops, where all but the heaviest work is done, are up beside the main line goods yard. Here were No's 1 (4-6-0T Hunslet 1912), 9 (2-6-2T Green 1898), 7 (4-6-0T Hunslet 1912), 11, (4-6-0T Bagnall 1909). No. 3 (4-6-0T Hunslet 1922) was on the goods and No.6 (another Dubs 0-6-2T) on the shuttle service between Kilkee and Kilrush. The locomotives are used turn and turn about as available. The goods turn is the heaviest working and often runs to 20 wagons.

After some tea, we left Ennis at 4.55pm on the daily train, having No. 5, two six wheelers and the Dingle bogie brake van. For the first time that day the rain had stopped and we hoped for better things. From Ennis the line runs northwards beside the main line to Athenry for a short distance. After crossing the River Fergus, the narrow gauge swings west, crosses the river again, and there is a fairly brisk run over straightish track to Corrofin (8.75 miles). A considerable speed was reached (I estimated about 40mph) and we rattled through some poor scrubby country with some small lakes and a considerable amount of flooding. A great deal was made of the whistle and, despite the flurry of No. 5's drivers, the running was very smooth. The Clare coaches, however, are not exactly the same acme of comfort, and are only 6ft 6in wide inside (compared with the Festiniog identical width on a smaller gauge of 2ft).

Once named *Ennistymon*, another Hunslet 4-6-0T, Class 'BN1', No. 3C built in 1922 works No. 1432, takes water at Ennis Junction on 28th September, 1931, adjacent to the dual purpose water tank. No's 3C and 7C were the last two locomotives built for an Irish narrow gauge railway and were regular performers in the latter years of the railway. [Photo: A.W. Croughton]

There was a long wait at Corofin owing to our early arrival, and the train effectively blocked the level crossing where numerous donkeys and scraggy horses, their two wheel carts piled high with turf, waited patiently. From Corofin the line rises consistently to its highest point and the watershed. We made a request stop at Willbrook (11.25 miles) a mere platform, and then ran twistily over some barren high ground down to Ennistymon (18.5 miles), the largest intermediate point. Here No. 3 on the goods was passed and we stopped for water. The rain had begun again, coming straight in off the Atlantic, now only a few miles to the west and, to complete the discomfiture, the compartment filled with wild Irish men and women, and we sat acutely squashed four per side.

A short run brought us to Lahinch (20.75 miles), a small seaside place with a station up above the beach. There are peculiar signals here governing the passing loop, one arm being fixed to the other on either side of a common post. The arm at clear shows the loop set for running, whilst that at danger shows the points are against that side.

From Lahinch the country becomes very poor indeed, in fact I have never seen anything in England to compare with the poverty of these parts. The land is rocky and infertile, and most of the cottages are but ill roofed with sprouting straw. To add to the misery of the scene the recent rains had flooded everywhere; the cattle stood in water from which there was

no escape. To complete the picture, a wet mist drove in from the sea, restricting visibility to a train length. The Irishmen puffed at their pipes, the women at their inevitable cigarettes; the men glared through the windows and the women at their muddied nylons. At one point en route the devout all crossed themselves, and the invisible barrier between race and creed could almost be seen. But it quickly faded. We were offered cigarettes, asked how much they were in England, what was the cost of beer....Soon we realised the friendly nature of the ever talkative Irishman and his generosity which, at times, could be great to the point of embarrassment.

At Miltown Mowbray (27 miles), after a spurt of speed, we made a long stop for water and the train emptied almost entirely, most of the passengers proving to be school children. The treeless upland continued to stretch on either hand, and for an hour we rose and fell through a most depressing vista which was not improved by the foggy weather. At Quilty (the place being but a few poor cottages on the Atlantic shore) the remains of the famous anemometer for measuring the velocity of the wind still stand. At the foot of the mast there is a small hut. The 'Spoons' from the top of the mast have disappeared and may have been put to exactly that purpose. We presume that the only remaining way of checking wind velocity is the time honoured Boy Scout method of holding up the wetted finger to the wind; but perhaps as all the passenger vehicles

3C, built in 1922, works No. 1432, stands at Milltown Mowbray with a train for Kilrush on 6th May, 1951, prior to the introduction of diesel railcars. Milltown Mowbray was the station at the end of the West Clare Railway from Ennis and the start of the South Clare Railway to Kilrush and Kilkee; in practice the entire line was always worked by the West Clare. The station had two passenger platforms, goods and cattle bays and a small engine shed. The first sod for the WCR was cut here on 26th January, 1885, although construction had actually already begun. [Photo: J.G. Dewing]

are now weighted with concrete slabs beneath the seats it is no longer necessary to send out gale warnings.

It was growing dusk as we drew up in the triangular junction at Moyasta (43 miles) and changed trains from that to Kilrush into the waiting No. 6 with its coach for Kilkee. Sister engines thus stood side by side in the dripping gloom and we, with no accommodation booked and a night sea behind us, could but think of another night in the open, or at best in a first class compartment in a very exposed siding. The trains moved off simultaneously, and we, the only passengers in the train, watched the Kilrush rake as it skirted along the opposite water's edge and the steam rose high in the damp air. Blackweir, a single platform beside the stone bridge over the creek, and then a long straight run through the barren treeless turf land to Kilkee (48 miles), a small but well appointed terminus some distance from the shore. The season was over, the holiday makers had returned to Limerick weeks ago, but the stationmaster showed the way and, despite our worst fears, we had an excellent night.

The train for Ennis leaves Kilkee at 8am. One of our most important items of luggage for this reason was an alarm clock as there is only one through train a day. At 7.55am the shed doors were opened and No. 6 wheezed out with the drain cocks spouting hot water. The whistle was opened – more hot water. The driver was still in bed and a runner was sent for him. Fortunately the fireman was there and it was a slight downhill run onto the coaches. At starting time the guard hustled me from the locomotive to a compartment, but I pointed out that it was unnecessary to be so upset when the pressure gauge read but 15lbs. Matters were soon put in order, and the whole train, engine and coach, gurgled off for Moyasta with 25lbs on the clock and a great cloud of wet steam ahead. The Ennis train, exactly the same as that of the previous day, was awaiting our arrival. Quite a number of people were going to Ennis and on to Limerick for the day and the brighter weather made the journey more pleasant. There are enough views of the rugged coastline from the train to whet the appetite for a much longer visit to these parts and no doubt the historian could have told us much of the well preserved castles which we saw from time to time. As the train drew near them, the rooks rose in force from the tops of the crumbling battlements.

At Ennis, the main line train gave us a pleasant run to Limerick through pastoral country in greatest contrast to that recently traversed. Limerick is quite a pretentious small

In 1891, George Hopkins (from the Midland Great Western Railway) designed a class of three 0-6-2Ts, *Slieve Callan*, *Saint Sennan* and *Lady Inchiquin* built by Dubs as Class 'IN1' for the South Clare Railway. Their names were removed by the Great Southern Railway on amalgamation in 1925. An interesting feature of these locomotives is the trailing wheelset, having wheels the same diameter as the coupled wheels in order to contain construction costs. Here No. 6C, formerly *Saint Sennan*, built in 1892, works No. 2891, stands at Ennis on 6th August, 1935.
[Photo: R.G. Jarvis]

No. 7C, a further Hunslet 4-6-0T to Class 'BN4' poses at Ennis Junction with the broad gauge in the background. With No. 3C the last two locomotives built for the Irish narrow gauge in 1922, works No's 1432/3. The Class 'BN4' feature Walschaerts valve gear, necessitating an alteration to the contour of the locomotives' water tanks.

Class 'PN1' and No. 9C, formerly *Fergus*, a 2-6-2T again designed by Hopkins as a class of four, but this time built by Thomas Green & Sons in Leeds in 1898, stands taking water at Ennis on 28th September, 1931. In order to obtain a better weight distribution, the locomotive's water tanks were extended to the middle of the smokebox. [Photo: A.W. Croughton]

terminus with all over roof and the accommodation for waiting passengers is very jaded, and this was forcibly brought home to us as we had a wait of five and a half hours for the daily train to Tralee.

On the following day, the Tralee & Dingle cattle special was due to leave in two portions, at 11 and 12 o'clock respectively. We duly reported 'for duty' and, as elsewhere, we were greeted and treated most cordially. We gathered the Dingle line was to be at our command for the day – or almost. What had promised to be a pleasant spot of sunshine turned into a torrential downpour before 10.30 am, so we repaired to the former station of the Dingle line which now appears to be a private house, and sheltered in the former booking office. Connection with the standard gauge goods yard is made through the streets of Tralee, there being an island platform in the main line sidings for the transfer of freight. Since the Tralee & Dingle section now operates but twelve times per year, the standard of maintenance has been allowed to fall and the track, rolling stock etc., though quite serviceable are not 'in the pink'.

Even in the hey day of passenger traffic, two and a half hours was allowed for the mountainous terrain of the narrow gauge

line with its banks of 1 in 24 and others little better. Today's little outing was expected to take at least three and a half hours running time. There are five locomotives on the Dingle section, being Hunslet 2-6-0 tanks No's 1, 2, 6 and 8; the fifth locomotive, No. 5, was up at Inchicore for a 'heavy'. For the monthly trip, four engines have to be steamed, meaning that each must be taken virtually 'out of store' for the purpose. The engines are now obliged to coal up from the island platform in the main goods yard, they take it in turn to run down the street for this purpose. It is not surprising that we were half an hour late getting away because of this. It should be mentioned that the engines are fitted with bells which once rang continuously (working off the motion), but now these are only rung as they pass through the streets of Tralee. Side casing and other tram like appurtenances have been removed these many years.

Our train consisted of pilot No. 8, train engine No. 1, one open wagon full of Cardiff briquettes, sixteen empty cattle vans, and the bogie guards van. Like all old T&D stock, the van had doors which opened inwards. The train was vacuum fitted and this was connected up (for once). We left Tralee for the distant mountains (which we were destined to cross) in a veritable cloudburst, but this did not damp the ardour. Neither

No. 10C, formerly *Lahinch*, a 4-6-0T built by Kerr Stuart in 1903, works No. 818, stands at Ennis works in the 1940s. [Photo: A.W. Croughton]

4-6-0T No. 11C stands at Ennis on 6th August, 1935. Formerly named *Kilkee* and built by Bagnalls in 1908, works No. 1881. [Photo: R.G. Jarvis]

Class 'BN3', No. 7C, formerly named *Malbay*, leaving Corrofin, the first staff section out of Ennis and 8.75 miles into the journey, with the afternoon train from Ennis and beginning the climb up to the wild moorland in May, 1950. [Photo: P.B. Whitehouse]

No. 6C 0-6-2T hurries towards Corrofin with an afternoon goods bound for Ennis in May, 1950. [Photo: P.B. Whitehouse]

Ennis Junction in May, 1950 with 4-6-0T No. 3C, formerly named *Ennistymon*, standing bunker first with a mixed train including two of the clerestory roofed tourist cars which were internally divided into two saloons. The locomotive is performing shunting moves for, apart from short trips between Kilkee and Kilrush, Irish practice was always for locomotives to run chimney first. [Photo: P.B. Whitehouse]

Ennis Junction looking south in May, 1950, showing both broad gauge line from Limerick to Tuam and the 3ft West Clare Section gauge lines. A Great Southern 0-6-0 takes water at the platform column with the broad gauge goods yard to the left. On the right of the picture is the single road engine shed of the WCR with wagons in the yard and a passenger train, including clerestory roofed tourist saloons, in the platform. Ennis was a prosperous market town with some 5,500 inhabitants and regarded as the gateway to County Clare. The town was the head office and works of the WCR. [Photo: P.B. Whitehouse]

Diesel railcar No. 3389 and its trailer shown on arrival at Kilkee with congratulations being given to the driver after a record non stop run from Ennis on 10th June, 1953. In the early 1950s, under C.I.E management, the West Clare Section began to use diesel traction. Passenger services were then largely operated by four new diesel railcars built by Walker Brothers of Wigan, England (almost identical in design to those used on the County Donegal Railway) and diesel locomotives for the freight traffic. [Photo: R.G. Jarvis]

did the stench in the van, part of which had been railed off for carrying cattle. It was in the centre of this portion that the handbrake screw was situated and, as the guard explained, *"how the devil could I be expected to apply the b_____ brake when the van was filled with b_____ cows and I had to b_____ well move them before I could turn the b_____ handle?"* We agreed. Incidentally, the crews on this monthly job are former Dingle section men. Main line men cannot be bribed into running this rake and though we looked surprised when told of this, on experience our sympathies are entirely with the main line men.

We made a good start from Tralee, whence the track runs on its own right of way for some miles. The two engines were belching clouds of steam into the damp air, but the rain eased off into a drizzle. Luckily the clouds were fairly high from here onward, and we did not miss the wonderful summits of some of the highest ranges in Ireland. At Blennerville (2.25 miles) the sea has been allowed to encroach onto the land and if the tide is high the train may have to run almost up to the axles in water. The running so far is level, and shortly the road is joined, the line running on either verge (usually to the north edge) until it gains its own right of way at Castlegregory Junction (or Lower Camp, as the men call it). As there is only

one platelayer per eight miles, the edges have grown so thick along this section that they almost came inside the van and swept us out. It made peering through the doorway a risky business. As the track follows the configuration of the road exactly, there are some tough banks and the leading engine was slipping quite a lot. This seemed to dry the rails for the second which never slipped at all. We jogged along thus for about an hour, occasionally being thrown to the floor when taken off our balance by a snatch in the coupling. Luckily no cows had been in this half of the van.

The guard informed us that there was a 10 minute scheduled stop at Castlegregory (10 miles) for the engines to take water, and so the *"engines and men are able to get a drink"*. *"Would you care for a drink, Boss?"* (I should add that I was 'Boss' throughout this trip). Little did we know that having arrived, we were due to remain for three and a half hours.

'Paddy' is the factotum at Castlegregory junction. He still accepts parcels etc., for the road lorries, and he was there to meet us and, being a conscientious man, the appropriate signals were pulled off. Paddy expected to join us in 'Fitzgerald's Bar' over the road, and never was a bar so well placed, I would think. However, all was not well at the water column where the stop cock was proving stubborn and though full 'on', not

Hunslet 2-6-0T No.2 outside the original Tralee engine shed in 1914. Note the brass number plate on the tank sides and the variety of goods vans and a cattle wagon with no roof in the train in the station. [Photo: K.R.C. Nunn]

Two Hunslet 2-6-0Ts under repair outside the Tralee workshops. On the left No. 1 is being rebuilt and on the right No. 3 is under repair after a collision in the station. [Photo: K.R.C. Nunn]

a solitary drip came from the hose. A conference was held around the spot and much good advice was given. Nothing was done. It was then suggested that water be taken from the tank, though this had not worked for 10 years. This was rather a dismal failure too. Adding to the misery, No. 1 was found to have a hot trailing box, and with half the train, was run into a siding in order to get it back to Tralee for repair. At 2pm, with still no luck with the stop tap, the various nabobs from Tralee arrived in a car, bringing a fitter, mate and the 'Plumber's Bag' with them. It was now obvious to us that Dingle would not be reached by the intended time, and that the bus to bring us back at 4.20pm would be well on its way before we got there. Not so good. The shed foreman, on his knees in the mud, and with water gushing up like a fountain, eventually succeeded in righting the bother and with the tanks of No. 8 completely dry, we were able to fill up in the nick of time.

After a conference with the foreman, it was decided to risk No. 1 with its hot box as there would be no time to run it back to Tralee, where the second portion had been unable to leave as they could not withdraw the tablet until ours had been handed over.

At 2.55pm we resumed our belated journey, leaving the junction at full blast to breast the long bank up to Glenagalt. Below us the course of the erstwhile Castlegregory line ran down to its roadside location, and the fields swept down to the

Atlantic shore in a graceful curve. Over the water was Fenit Harbour and the County Limerick coast. To the west the mountains fell sharply into the sea, their summits in mist, with the small thatched cottages, like white spots on their flanks. This was the beginning of what is undoubtedly the worst bank on any railway in these islands. Here we were hours behind time, the rails wet with rain and bent grass, and one of the engines had a hot box! The guard was more than pessimistic and told us grim tales of divided trains and stalling engines. He pointed out the derelict two stone arched viaduct at Camp now by passed, with its treacherous approach curve where, in the early years of the line, a pig train had careered out of control down the bank and pitched over the side of the bridge, killing the crew, the locomotive superintendent, and most of the pigs as well.

But we were going surprisingly well, I thought. The guard did not. The two little engines snaked round the long bend in front, nosing along the hillside like small dogs in the gutter, crossed the later built steel bridge and cut through the hillside to join the old course again. There followed a long exciting grind along the verge of the road, collar work all the way, a sinuous bank of two miles with a bleak valley running down to the shore below, and the wild hills all around us. There was never anything like this on any narrow gauge line in England or Wales, though Skye might have provided scenery for one. Speed dropped quickly, every now and then one of the locomotives would slip and we wondered how the hot box was doing. I nearly fell out trying to get photos of the huge smokepall we were making. For all I knew the engines might be full of steam and the men full of Irish whiskey, but there was precious little water in the boilers and the men were as thirsty as their charges when we reached the old passenger platform at Glenagalt (13.75 miles), and allowed the steam into the injectors. The guard was jubilant and insisted that we had knocked ten minutes off the running time from the Junction. True or not we had certainly added to our store of narrow gauge experiences, if nothing else.

For the long run down the hill (680ft above sea level here) which extends with smaller undulations to the next passing loop at Annascaul, the guard was very insistent that we should have adequate brake availability. The vacuum brake gauge showed but ten inches. "*Tap the glass, Boss?*" he said. Eleven inches. The guard came over and smote the glass in a way no barometer could tolerate, but it held. The needle flicked to fifteen and we started. The train began to push the engines which led us down a long bleak mountain valley with peat bogs to the south, and occasional glimpses though the mountain passes of Dingle Bay and the Atlantic. We were now in the heart of the Slieve Mish and it would be difficult to describe the wildness of the countryside. On a clear day it is possible to see the steam of the Valencia Harbour branch train as it runs along the south shore of Dingle Bay. The guard was getting upset again for the vacuum had dropped to nothing, but with the aid of a herdsman (there were several passengers in the van) managed to get the handbrake full on. It seemed to

make little difference and we shot over ungated level crossings in a manner which would make me a most careful motorist in these parts. Eventually, reaching the roadside again and still running through poor but wild scenery we ran quickly down a steep grade into Annascaul (21.25 miles), barefoot children running in the wet street to meet us from school, and many stray animals narrowly avoiding mincemeat. Finally, we abandoned the road, and crossing over the Owenascaul River, entered the loop and former island platform station where both engines took water and, as at Corofin, two days earlier, effectively blocked the level crossings where in next to no time, and seemingly from nowhere, the inevitable donkey carts with peat were queuing.

From Annascaul, where the stop was quite lengthy to enable engines and men, once again, to partake of liquid refreshment, the railway leaves the company of the road to take a more inland course and climb to a considerable height once more, this time along the southern outflanks of Ireland's second mountain, Brandon Hill (3,127ft.). The scenery continues to be of the finest, there being little habitation and no trees at all. The railway route from Annascaul, whilst climbing first, and then descending to Lispole, abounds in short dips and sharp curves, which are all the more appreciated from the footplate.

It had been impossible to carry three on the engine until this point as well over half the cab was full of coal (this is necessary because fuel has to be carried for the return run also). After Annascaul most of this had been used up, and with a very cheery crew I settled down behind the driver for a monumental trip. The driver, the image of Victor MacLagen, put me in mind of that actor's *The Informer*, but nothing could I

Hunslet 2-6-0T No. 6 on the 8.30am mixed train in Tralee station platform in 1925. Note the open roofed cattle wagon behind the engine and the carriages in the middle of the train, made possible by the railway's use of vacuum brake. [Photo: H.L. Hopwood]

No's 1 and 2 double head an empty cattle train over Lispole viaduct on their way to Dingle on 29th April, 1938. From the 1920s, the GSR civil engineer would not permit double heading over this viaduct, due to its condition. Normally, the crew observed this restriction on the way out, detaching the pilot engine and running it across the viaduct light engine, to be recoupled to the rest of the train once it too had crossed the viaduct. In this picture, however, the crew have ignored the rule, but for no good reason. On the return runs, however, the restriction was ignored more often than not. The crew did not want to stop and then have to restart a heavy train on the steep gradient which starts in the middle of the viaduct. And they were keen to get home!

make of anything the driver 'informed' me – as on the previous day, the clatter and the rich accent were too much. I hope I nodded in the right places.

For the initial climb, from the start, full gear and half regulator was used, and speed controlled throughout by use of the reversing screw. We slipped considerably on the grass grown rails, clearing the track for the following engine which, again, never slipped at all. The brickettes have a peculiar odour when burning, more like the native turf, and this blew around as we bellowed up the bank. There is no rear bunker on these engines and, leaning through the square window in the back sheet, I could almost lean out and touch the chimney of No. 1. At the summit the regulator was eased, and I looked back at a long string of vans and the brake van, coming through a trough of bracken. The rails were quite invisible.

It would be difficult to describe the sensation as we rolled down the bank, the train engine still working and we being propelled. There was a bad knock on the rod somewhere under my feet and, at every revolution, the floor jolted vertically, and at the same time, lurched sideways (there is a big rear overhang) at each lurch the cab door, with its fastening broken, clanged against the tank side. The cut off too, being somewhat excessive to ease steaming, imparted the well known forward backward see saw motion to the locomotive, and the combined effect of these gymnastics was sufficient to numb the brain at high speed.

I soon got used to the motion but the speed was at times

more than I could wish for. It was still raining quite hard and looking backward it was striking the chimney and smokebox behind me and darting off in spurts of steam. The following engine presented a peculiar appearance as the chimney and dome literally grew out of a heap of briquettes and firewood on the boiler barrel. Now and then the driver would lean right out and point out some landmark or particularly fine piece of coast and mountain scenery down below us. As we neared the summit the din became greater, and the see sawing reached a pitch. Looking over the rear of the engine the gap between the two locomotives yawned to and fro and the motion of No. 1's cowcatcher showed how little did the engine follow the intended course of the rails. We topped the summit at about 5mph, blowing off at 150lbs. on both locomotives, and the fireman throwing down the shovel and opening the firedoor slightly as we began to coast down the severe and winding hill to the Lispole viaduct at the foot.

Driver and fireman both pulled at the hand screw. The vacuum brake was then fully applied, but still we rushed on. It was quite obvious that on the wet rails the train was pushing us. With each successive bend I thought of the poor standard of maintenance which this section of track receives, and hardened "footplater" though I may be, could not admit to a feeling of apprehension as the curves ground beneath us and we lurched over first to one side then the other. The train followed like a writhing serpent and with a last squeal we entered the first portion of Lispole viaduct, the driver pointing

In May, 1953, No. 8T stands inside the forlorn Tralee engine shed. [Photo: Dave Waldren Collection]

On 11th June, 1953, the Light Railway Transport League chartered a two coach passenger train over the Tralee & Dingle, with station seats and benches put aboard the two vans which had been converted to carry cattle in about 1942. Here 2-6-0T, No. 8T, which was to be the last engine in use on the line, stands in Dingle station with the League's headboard on its smokebox ready for the return journey. Local kids have piled in to the first van for their first and only train ride out of Dingle and the crew kindly took them for a ride for about half a mile along the mail road and then back again. [Photo: R.G. Jarvis]

to the former course of the line from whence an uncontrollable train had leapt into the river bed.

There is a dip in the middle of the Lispole viaduct, marking the bottom of the decline, and then the line climbs through the small station at the roadside (27.5 miles). There is no passing loop. A short distance further on the last summit is reached, and in front there stretches a bleak open vista of country, sloping to the sea. In a few yards the railway joins the northern edge of the road and, passing through the outer edges of several farmyards, begins the 'long straight'. This is almost two miles of dreary road, dead straight, with a smaller declivity in the bottom. Here the grass and overgrown hedges were most abundant, but fortunately wheel slip did not matter hereabouts. More dangerous were the numbers of cattle, their drovers unable to guide them, which thronged the road and wandered at will over the track in front of us. All these were on the way to the fair, and some had walked many miles. Their drovers indifferent to merciless drizzle which still fell. It was wretchedly cold, too, though on the footplate it was warm enough.

At the further end of the 'straight,' the line cut crazily over the road at a sharp angle, and breasting the summit of a small rise, we saw the whole sweep of landlocked Dingle Bay and the harbour below us. It was a delightful setting, but hardly in the same weather conditions as had pertained when photographs

which hang, framed, in the porch of Brenner's Hotel, Tralee, were taken. The final mile into Dingle is treacherous with blind corners and the steep hill, running as it does along the road until the terminus is reached. The brakes were fully applied and we literally skidded all the way. The nearer we got to the station, the worse the numbers of cattle on the road became, and several might never have reached the fair at all but for some timely lumps of briquette shied from the footplate.

Dingle at last – six hours from Tralee and 32 odd miles away. No time was lost in putting the train into the cattle docks for the morning, turning and coaling the engines and putting them away in the little shed. There were one or two farewell photographs, and then the men were away to their billets, carrying potatoes, onions, frying pans and all the impedimentia of a portable kitchen with them. The silence of the past four weeks fell – as did the rain – on the station, now ready to receive the second portion of the special.

After briefly noting the grassgrown track of the now disused extension down to the harbour, we climbed aboard a C.I.E lorry and trailer which the authorities, with the thoughtfulness which had pervaded our whole journey, had kept waiting for us. It was dark and we were mighty wet when the lights of Tralee came into sight, but the ambition of months was accomplished.

Pat Whitehouse took this sequence of photographs in July, 1951 of No's 1T & 2T double heading a cattle train for the monthly Dingle fair

No. 1T, as pilot engine, double heads No. 2T, the train engine, on the monthly empty stock for the Dingle fair standing in Tralee station platform. No. 2T is having its motion oiled but, otherwise, the train is ready to depart as the crew have now been paid. Note the pile of briquettes in front of 1T's smokebox door; the locomotives had to take enough coal to get to Dingle and back! The carriage & wagon shops are behind the train.

No's 1T & 2T stand at Castlegregory Junction having taken water at the standpipe behind No. 1T. Both locomotives are being checked and oiled. The junction station was the first watering point for both men and machines; Fitzgerald's bar is just across the road and it is still there with memorabilia on the walls and a piece of rail in use as a footstool at the bar counter. Note the water tower towards the back of the train which is also still standing.

No's 1T & 2T climbing up to Camp en route to Skirlough; one of the steepest grades on the Irish narrow gauge. This picture shows the typical scenery on a 'soft' Irish day with the mountains in the background and the roadway alongside which the railway ran for most of its length, darting across and back many times over open crossings which, in times past, resulted in many accidents to both cars and horses and carts and even a circus!

The infamous Glenagalt bank with No's 1T and 2T giving their all to get the train over the summit at the 'Place of the Mad'. As, by then, trains only ran monthly, the track was often rusty and damp which did not help adhesion, particularly for the pilot engine which used to slip and clean the rails, enabling the train engine to grip firmly. Although the construction of the line was done to a budget, which resulted in steep climbs, switchbacks and roadside running, the Hunslet six coupled tank engines were made of sturdy stuff and, when in good condition, were very capable machines.

No's 1T and 2T pause for an unscheduled wayside stop as the driver inspects the valve gear of 2T, the train engine. 'PBW' seized the opportunity of an extra shot during the car chase before continuing on to get ahead for the next shot, leapfrogging the train all the way to Dingle.

No's 1T & 2T ready to depart Annascaul, the second water stop on the way to Dingle. In the middle distance behind and above the train can be seen the main road from Tralee to Dingle.

At Dingle 1T has just come off the shed ready to couple up to 2T, the train engine, standing with the returning cattle train in Dingle station. The overall roof still remains as part of a funeral parlour. Interestingly, Tralee station building also remains and is also a funeral parlour!

Chapter Five

Memories of the Monorail
By Pat Whitehouse
[Extracted from Narrow Gauge Album]

The old gymnasium hall was packed to the doors, for the showing of a film in those far off days of the immediate post-1914 war era was an occasion, especially so in north west Kerry, where there could have been few, if any, of the cinemas so readily taken for granted today. But this evening was a special show, a film in which many of the local people had participated and, above all, its hero was none other than the Lartigue itself, an innovation peculiar to Listowel and its seaside neighbour, Ballybunion.

That the railway (for what else could it be called?) had achieved fame, there was no doubt, for its construction was entirely unique in the British Isles. The track was not laid in the ordinary fashion along the ground, neither was it a railway line, in the normal sense of the term, for the contraption was a monorail whose track was supported on a metal trestle 3ft high, below which ran two guide rails 2ft 4in under the running rail, the whole, in section, representing a capital A. The weight of the main rail was 27lb per yard. Steel plates were fixed to the foot of the supports, these resting on wooden sleepers or, on boggy ground, upon two timber baulks. The inventor of the system, after whom it was named, claimed a great saving in cost over conventional methods of railway building and, indeed, this was so, for the units could be prefabricated and then assembled on site. The figure quoted for this nine and a quarter mile line was £3,300 per mile.

The line had been opened for traffic in 1888, unwisely without that normal safeguard of the Irish Light Railway, the Baronial Guarantee, for the traffic which its promoters had so rosily foreseen did not materialise and a Receiver was appointed as early as 1897. The locomotives and stock resembled giant donkey panniers, the centre of which lay on the top rail and travelled along it, whilst hidden in the sides were two small transverse wheels running along the guide rails below. The original locomotive was a strange machine with twin vertical boilers about which there appears to be little authentically recorded. This was followed by three others, this time built by the Hunslet Engine Company and having twin locomotive boilers disposed on either side of the main rail and projecting from a central cab. The whole equipage was

Irish to the last bolt, the final touches being the railed flight of steps on wheels which were marshalled into the train to allow the passengers to cross the line. The vision of these being appropriately shunted can be left to the imagination.

This was the scene which had greeted two enterprising cameramen on arrival at Listowel, where they eventually settled down and opened their first cinema. Meanwhile, they had duly shot a two reel film of the Lartigue and their audience was now anxiously awaiting the appearance of the line, together with pictures of themselves, fathers, brothers, uncles and cousins on the flickering screen. As a pianist and fiddler had been engaged as an overture to the show, the crowd were already beginning to enjoy themselves, tackling a local chorus with gusto.

"The old train's held together with rope
And the tacking, they say, won't endure, sir,
Sure they balance the people with soap,
And sometimes with bags of manure, sir."

At last the lights were dimmed and the film came onto the screen. The crowd went wild at seeing themselves on a moving picture, creating such a disturbance that the pianist and fiddler had to give up the unequal struggle and join in the howling mob.

There was plenty for them to see and a visitor would have been intrigued by the novelty of the whole thing, for such a monorail necessitated many innovations, apart from the staircases on wheels. There were, for example, the peculiar methods of road and rail crossings. At each major road crossing there was a drawbridge raised by pulleys, the floor of the bridge being connected to cross-bar type signals indicating danger to the railway when the road vehicle had right of way. Minor roads and occupation crossings were served by a small section of the railway on hinges, thus converting it into a gate. These gates were protected in a similar manner to the drawbridges.

Had this film been made with a sound track, it might well have overcome the competition of the noisy crowd, for both the locomotives and the stock oscillated considerably when

An overall view of Ballybunion station with a train of carriages on the left hand track and one of the locomotives standing in the platform road. Note the horizontal back board positioned for the protection of the 'rotating switch.'
[Photo: National Library. Dublin]

The main line near Teampaillin bridge, just outside Listowel with the Thoumplebawn burial ground on the right which contains a memorial to the victims of the Great Famine. The running rail was in 33ft lengths weighing 27lbs per yard. It was secured to the apex of 'A' shaped iron trestles sited about 3ft apart anchored to steel or timber sleepers, depending on the ground conditions. Secured to the outer face of each trestle were lighter horizontal rails of 11lb per yard, the running surfaces of which faced outwards, their object being to stabilize the rolling stock rather than carry any weight. The inner sides of the locomotives and carriages had double flanged wheels which bore against these rails.
[Photo: National Library, Dublin]

No. 3 stands with its train in Ballybunion station: passenger coach, step car, passenger coach and three sea sand wagons. There were three locomotives on the line, all built by Hunslets of Leeds in 1887, Works No's 431, 432 & 433. All were painted dark green.
[Photo: National Library, Dublin]

running and it is said that the coaches, during their latter days especially, set up a nerve-racking drumming in the ears of the passengers, who were unpleasantly close to the running rail.

The Lartigue, due to the fact that it was unique, brought many people to visit and travel upon it, the little town of Ballybunion attracting a great number of tourists, especially in the years just prior to the First World War. Though at the time of its closing in 1925, there were but three trains a day, a peculiarity of this timetable being the fact that, although the locomotive shed was at Listowel, the first train was scheduled out of Ballybunion and the last terminated there.

Most of the trains were mixed, for one of the original reasons for the building of the line was the desire to transport large quantities of Ballybunion sea sand, which contained a high phosphate content. This was either used locally or transferred from a high level siding into the waiting wagons of the Irish broad gauge at Listowel. There was originally only one intermediate station, Lisselton, which was carefully set out as a passing loop, though latterly the line was operated on the 'one engine' or 'two boilers' in steam principle. The summer excursions were probably the mainstay of the line and these, of course, originated at Listowel, mainly in connection with the broad gauge trains.

The Troubles really precipitated the end for, during that time, considerable damage was done to the stock, damage which an insolvent company could not afford to repair.

The final straw was the refusal of the Irish Government to include the system in the Great Southern Railways merger. On 14th October, 1924, the line was closed by Order of the High Court, having been in the Receiver's hands for 27 years.

The Lartigue is still spoken of with a mixture of laughter and sentiment at Listowel and, even after thirty years, tourists were still able to obtain picture postcards of the railway, both at Listowel and in Ballybunion. Every now and again, a local newspaper runs an article to revive its memory and, once again, the flickering picture on the screen is revived in mens' minds for a short while.

The very last word should be left to the, probably apocryphal and certainly exaggerated, story of the farmer who had bought a cow at the Listowel fair, who had to borrow another to enable his beast to be carried by rail to Ballybunion to balance the load on the monorail. On arrival, another cow was needed, to facilitate the return of the first one borrowed. This procedure continued for a little time, cattle shuttling two and fro, until the farmer had lost one cow and paid the price of his own beast in freight charges in his efforts to avail of the railway livestock service! A probably truer tale concerns the Ballybunion lady, who had purchased a piano in the days before large motor vans were available. When the instrument arrived at Listowel, the same problem arose; however, this was overcome by placing two calves in the wagon on the other side of the monorail, animals and piano then travelling safely to Ballybunion.

Locomotive No. 1 and a train, including carriages A1, A2 and A5, followed by a step car and then at least another carriage, stand at Ballybunion with the locomotive crew posing on the tender and Mr Patrick McCarthy, the Manager (and Receiver), in front of the locomotive.
[Photo: National Library, Dublin]

BALLYBUNION RAILWAY. Co.KERRY. 9852.W.L.

View of Ballybunion station with engine shed far left, 4 ton goods wagon on spur siding, steam locomotive about to enter the rotating switch having arrived with a mixed train which stands in the station (sea sand wagons attached to the rear). [Photo: National Library, Dublin]

Similar (but earlier) view, showing the rotating switch section set for the run round loop and a passenger train in Ballybunion station getting ready for the journey to Listowel.
[Photo: National Library, Dublin]

The only passing loop on the line at Lisselton, 4.5 miles from Listowel, with a train of four carriages, a step car and third brake van in the station. A siding can be seen radiating from the near rotating switch. A curious family group peer out of the open doorway in their cottage and post office to the right. [Photo: National Library, Dublin]

Bill O'Reilly standing on the fireman's side of locomotive No. 1 as it moves off the rotating switch prior to backing down onto the train in the station, watched by Joe Holyoake leaning on a siding rail. The locomotive crew stood one on each side of the monorail and were obliged to drive and fire the engine on their side of the track. [Photo: National Library, Dublin]

A train on the line near Teampaillin bridge, just outside Listowel. [Photo: National Library, Dublin]

Side view of a mixed train behind locomotive No. 1 featuring composite coach (one first and two third class sections), two door third class coach, three door first class coach, a set of mobile steps and a guard's van with third and first class sections and six sea sand wagons at the rear. Note the guard's van compartment has a 'birdcage' overall roof having windows at the top so the guard can look both forward and rear

[Photo: Irish Record Society]

Locomotive No. 1 and passenger train stands at Listowel station around 1924 (some three years before closure) with the driver making some adjustments on top of the locomotive. The broad gauge station and a signal can be seen in the background.

Locomotive No. 1 stands in Listowel station on 31st May, 1924 with a mixed train for Ballybunion. [Photo: A.W. Croughton]

Front and side views of locomotive No. 1 on the turntable at Listowel locomotive depot and repair shops on 31st May, 1924 with Mr. Paddy Boyle standing by the side of the locomotive. On the cabside can be seen the brass numberplate with the locomotive number and the railway company's initials. The tender carried a plate with the inscription: 'Lartigue Single-Rail System Mallet's Patent.' [Photo: A.W. Croughton]

The monorail suffered from incursions during the Troubles, like many of the other Irish railways, but never really recovered from the Civil War damage shown here after the Francis Road accident on 26th January, 1923.

4-4-0 No. 8 At Ballinamore with a train for Dromod on 11th May, 1924. The Cavan & Leitrim Railway ordered eight 4-4-0Ts from Robert Stephenson & Sons of Newcastle upon Tyne all built in 1887. No. 8 had works No. 2619 and was named *Queen Victoria*. [Photo: A.W. Croughton]

Chapter Six

The Last Entirely Steam Operated Narrow Gauge Railway in Ireland
By Pat Whitehouse
[Extracted from On The Narrow Gauge]

The last entirely steam operated narrow gauge railway in Ireland was the Cavan & Leitrim section of the CIE It started life as the Cavan, Leitrim and Roscommon Light Railway & Tramway Co. Ltd. and began to operate in 1887; true to the tradition of most of its brethren it managed to have a serious accident before it opened, though it must be acknowledged that its later record was excellent. This accident happened to one of the contractor's trains on 15th March, 1887 and unfortunately killed three men. The train was returning from Fenagh towards Mohill in the evening and it was dark. After unloading the four wagons of sand at Clooncahir, the engine propelled them down the line in the direction of Mohill. About 200 yards beyond the crossing they ran into an ass, and all the wagons were derailed, throwing the men riding on them in all directions; no-one escaped serious injury. What happened to the ass is not recorded.

It is often thought that the well known Arigna branch was the original *raison d'être* for the Cavan & Leitrim, but this was not so and, indeed, the final extension of this branch was only opened as late as 1920. The real reason for the

Robert Stephenson built 4-4-0T Class 'DN2' No. 1 *Isabel* on Ballinamore engine shed, buffered up to former Cork Blackrock & Passage 2-4-2T No. 12L. The class were generally named after daughters of the directors and *Isabel* was named after the daughter of R.H. Johnstone, the longest serving director.

line's construction was cattle and such towns as Ballyconnel, Ballinamore, Drumshambo and Mohill were important cattle trading centres – one only had to appear at Ballinamore on a fair day to find that out. However, it was the coal traffic which grew to be the mainstay of the Cavan & Leitrim, and this was particularly so during the Second World War with its cessation of supplies of British coal to Ireland. The section shared the doubtful privilege with the broad gauge Castlecomer branch of being one of Ireland's only coal railways.

For many years the Arigna coal, which was of poor enough quality by most standards, was in heavy demand by certain sugar factories, but with the restoration of supplies from 'over the water' this demand dwindled and finally ceased. Later, despite frequent strikes in the mines and consequent spasms of inactivity when the daily mixed train to Ballinamore was adequate and more to deal with the demand, a new contract was arranged with a cement company.

This was initially for a factory at Drogheda necessitating the running of coal specials for the first time over the Ballinamore to Belturbet section, and later for the Castlemungret factory via the Ballinamore to Dromod line. In both cases, of course,

transshipment was necessary to the broad gauge lines of the Great Northern and CIE respectively.

Despite the fact that it was coal traffic which prolonged the life of the Cavan & Leitrim, its original purpose of carrying cattle was fulfilled to the end. Cattle sold at various fairs up and down the line had a two way outlet afforded by connections at Belturbet towards Belfast and Dromod towards Dublin but, in practice, most went out via Belturbet. The fairs at Mohill were probably the largest, particularly those in October and February – for some unaccountable reason the latter was always known as 'Monaghen Fair'. On these occasions and when the coal traffic was heavy, the railway's resources were taxed to the utmost. This heavy traffic and the ravages of time brought the Cavan & Leitrim a heterogeneous collection of locomotives and rolling stock.

By the time the Great Southern took over the line in 1925 the original stock was practically 40 years old and it had been worked pretty hard. The engines supplied to the line on opening were all 4-4-0 tanks supplied by Robert Stephenson & Co. and there were eight of them. All were named after ladies. There was No. 1 *Isabel*, No. 2 *Kathleen*, No. 3 *Lady Edith*, No. 4

Robert Stephenson built 4-4-0T No. 3 *Lady Edith* seen here on 17th May, 1924 in fully lined out green livery. The lining colours varied between locomotives, depending on the whim of the locomotive superintendent or the painter. This locomotive was bought for preservation by Edgar T. Mead's consortium and exported to the U.S.A. when the railway closed, along with Tralee & Dingle 2-6-2T No. 5T. [Photo: A.W. Croughton]

4-4-0T No. 8 *Queen Victoria*, with nameplate removed, at Ballinamore on 17th May, 1924 . She lost her name in 1923 under what were tactfully described as 'patriotic circumstances'. Driver Jonny Gaffney, deciding that as the country was then independent, visited the sheds one Sunday afternoon and removed the offending nameplates making quite a noise whilst doing so. Fitter in charge, Joe Shanks, knew better than to interrupt this important work. The plates were buried in the yard where, some months later, they were found by the stationmaster's son. The railway decreed that the plates should be restored and so this was reluctantly carried out. However, within a couple of days Barney Leddy took No. 8 to Drumshambo where the plates came off again, this time for good. [Photo: A.W. Croughton]

Violet, No. 5 *Gertrude*, No. 6 *May*, No. 7 *Olive* and No. 8 *Queen Victoria*. It is thought that these names were mostly the names of wives and daughters of the first directors of the railway, *Queen Victoria* being most specially excepted. *Gertrude, May, Olive* and *Queen Victoria* (of course) had decently long skirts over their wheels to allow them to run on the Arigna branch which was a roadside tramway and to conform with the Board of Trade Regulations. These engines did yeoman service and some were still at work when the line finally closed.

In 1904 a larger locomotive arrived at Ballinamore; this was No. 9 *King Edward*, an 0-6-4 tank with its frames in two parts! The main frames, 14ft 5in long, were, as usual, inside the coupled wheels, but behind these the hind frames 11ft 4in long were 4ft 2in apart instead of 2ft 5.5in, so allowing a much larger firebox. No. 9 was provided during the more prosperous years when the company were considering extensions, but proved too heavy for the track and was not extensively used. It was withdrawn in 1934 after doing little work.

By 1934 two of the 4-4-0s (No's 5 and 6) had also gone to

Valhalla and the locomotive situation was grim. Fortunately, the Cork, Blackrock & Passage line had closed in 1932 and four engines from here transferred to Ballinamore. These were 2-4-2 tanks built by Neilson & Co in 1899. They had 4ft 6in driving wheels and were capable of a decidedly good turn of speed. They were CB & P No's 4, 5, 6 and 7, and were renumbered 10L, 11L, 12L and 13L. The Arigna branch was prohibited to them after initial trials when they spread the track at the curves, but they proved excellent machines for the main line services. An indication of their popularity on passenger and livestock trains can be seen by their average weekly mileage of 1,000; which isn't bad considering that the total distance from Dromod to Belturbet was only 33.75 miles.

The next arrivals came from the Tralee & Dingle when No's 3T and 4T descended on Ballinamore in 1942. This was at a time of acute national coal shortage and, during this emergency period, Arigna coal, as bad as it was, became in great demand throughout Eire. Both the Dingle engines were 2-6-0 tanks, though 3T was the larger, being one of that railway's standard

Hunslet designs; 4T was a Kerr Stuart of smaller design. Shortly after this there was yet another arrival from Tralee in the shape of No. 5T, a 2-6-2T, again built by Hunslet and the largest running on the Cavan & Leitrim since the departure of *King Edward*. As late as 1957 there followed yet another Tralee & Dingle engine, this time No. 6T which had spent four years on the West Clare section. These engines from the far south west gave good service though, because of their shallow ashpans, they did not take very kindly to the Arigna coal with its high ash content. A point of interest is that, whilst the Tralee & Dingle drivers gave a very bad account of the Kerr Stuart, which they described as "useless." The Ballinamore men liked her better than 3, 5 or 6, hence she was worked very hard. The explanation of the Tralee & Dingle men's dislike of her may lie in the Cavan & Leitrim men's one criticism - her brakes were weak, a serious enough disadvantage on the latter line, but quite fatal on the Tralee & Dingle. As an aside, quite in keeping with the nature of the Irish narrow gauge, it is said that when the Tralee & Dingle inquiry before closure was being held certain figures were put forward to show the loss on working the line. Amongst these figures were the cost of working the engines, and it has been said that those engines which were already at Ballinamore were still being debited to the Tralee & Dingle.

It was depressing to see the Cavan & Leitrim in its last years, its engines were generally filthy inside as well as out and, with the exception of 6T, which had been done up at Inchicore in 1957, were in poor condition. Its coaches were little better and in some cases it was obvious that their bodies had been crudely repaired just to keep the sides vertical – one was even rebodied with an assemblage of old bus parts. At the time of closure there were but five coaches serviceable, the converted bus No. 7L, two open ended bogie coaches, 5L and 6L, an ex Tralee & dingle coach (in good condition) 21L and a rebuilt Cavan & Leitrim bogie coach 1L. There were, however, two saving graces – the condition of the track which was excellent, and the spirit of the men.

The last day of working was 31st March, 1959 and it was 6T which bore the brunt of that day – she was the only engine in what could be termed reasonable condition. Service began with the 8am Ballinamore to Dromod, where the Cavan & Leitrim connected with the old Midland Great Western Railway. Here it waited for the diesel from Dublin, 80 or so miles away, and this arrived punctually at 11.52

'Watch the birdie!' A carefully posed image of the locomotive crew, station staff and local kids gathered on the footplate and cow catcher of No. 8, formerly *Queen Victoria*, at Dromod on 17th May, 1924. The driver has been asked to hold the headlamp and the fireman to touch the lubricator whilst looking ahead. The Irish lads are most probably fascinated by the English photographer; had they ever seen such antics before? Maybe they liked the idea the engine had been de-named and the photographer was recording the fact? [Photo; A. W Croughton]

4-4-0T No. 8 on the turntable at Ballinamore engine shed now bereft of original lined livery as well as nameplates.

The train crew pose for the photographer at Ballinamore as 4-4-0 No. 2 *Kathleen* prepares to leave with a mixed train.

bringing with it the inevitable hoard of 'last day' travelling enthusiasts. Among these were included visitors from as far afield as Glasgow and Hampshire, not forgetting a priest in a flowing cassock which proved little hindrance when it came to positioning for photography.

By then 6T had been turned and backed down to the head of four bogie coaches, each apparently older than the next. There were also two vans in case the overflow of passengers made these necessary. The four passenger coaches, representing 80 per cent of the section's serviceable vehicles, consisted of the best of the lot, one being the Tralee & Dingle compo. The crowd lost no time in looking for relics of the older days – they were not hard to find for the wagons scattered about the sidings must have come from every narrow gauge line to come into the hands of the Great Southern Railway.

At 12.20 the driver got the 'green' and the cloud of briquette smoke which had clothed the narrow gauge bay became even worse as 6T moved off at a brisk pace towards Mohill and Ballinamore, where it arrived at 2pm, the time it was due away to Belturbet!

After a shunt, and the acquisition of some vitally needed water, 6T was off again with two coaches and some wagons to Belturbet an hour late – most of the passengers had opted for the Arigna branch train due out at 1.50pm. Belturbet platform was thronged with people and, to add to the confusion, a wagon

load of sheep was attached to the return train for dropping off at Ballyconnell. The 4.20pm train for Ballinamore left at 5.30pm, to the accompaniment of the usual fog signals, finally reaching Ballinamore at 6.25pm when the whole station and its environs were packed with humanity.

Meanwhile 5T had set off for Arigna at 2.33pm complete with two open ended bogie coaches, 5L and 6L (taken off the morning train from Dromod) plus five wagons. Even this late start was only managed by the staff rounding up the intended passengers who were widely scattered about Ballinamore yards poking around for items of interest. By dint of much whistling all were assembled and the 'Right Away' given by the genial sandy haired guard, whose instructions to the driver were 'Stop everywhere, Paddy.' Stops were made at all the hedge halts down the line, for photographic purposes both by the passengers and by the posse of motorists who were following the train. There was even a purple skirted lady who knelt in the road to obtain the required low angle shots. So, flanked by outriders, the train steamed into Drumshambo where a tape recorder was playing Irish folk music and a vociferous local inhabitant distributed leaflet describing the attractions of the neighbourhood at the same time forecasting doom when the line closed. The wagons were dropped off here – it would have been impossible to shunt them with the two coaches so jammed with people.

4-4-0T No. 3L, formerly *Lady Edith*, returning to Arigna with coal empties on the 3.25pm service from Ballinamore on 28th June, 1939.
[Photo: P.W. Gray]

Arigna was reached three quarters of an hour late at 4pm and here 5T needed the protection of the local Garda to reach the turntable and turn. In view of the late arrival, the guard decided that the return would be at 4.24pm and not at 4.15pm as advertised, and this welcome relief enabled 5T's driver to attend to the nuts on her piston gland which had been blowing all the way up, despite attention during 'photographic stops.' The train left, to shouts, cheers and detonations, and after 15 minutes arrived at Drumshambo where a local councillor harangued the crowd for five minutes or so, making repeated references to the days of independence. After some presentations the train got under way once more at 5.15pm; it was now 37 minutes late, which wasn't bad considering that the wagons left behind on the outward journey had to be shunted and water taken as well. Once again stops were made at all the halts where the local people had turned out to cheer the train on its way, and a further half an hour was lost before reaching Ballinamore. The arrival almost coincided with that of the 4.50pm from Dromod which came in behind 4T complete with the Tralee & Dingle compo and a motley collection of vans and wagons. The only Cavan & Leitrim engine in steam was 4L shunting in the yard.

The last rites were due to begin at 7pm with the departure of the final train to Dromod, and this eventually left at 7.38pm with the whole of the passenger stock still able to run. The train was double headed by 4T and 5T and all the coaches were crammed to the end platforms with people – all the way along the line people turned out to pay their tribute – and Dromod was reached just under an hour late due to the accompaniment of the town band. The 6pm Dublin to Sligo railcar gave long blasts on its klaxon horn as did the 7.30pm Sligo-Dublin diesel electric, and 4T and 5T replied with their whistles. Both engines were turned and eventually the 8.40pm left for Ballinamore just over an hour late accompanied by much noise and cheering and shouting. In a way it was reminiscent of the closing of the Lynton & Barnstaple for, despite heavy rain, there were small crowds at all the halts and stations who had come to bid their own railway farewell. Ballinamore was reached at 11.08pm well over an hour and 20 minutes late, and here the whole town must have turned out. The coaches were left in the platform and the engines quietly moved off to the shed; the Drumshambo councillor once again harangued the crowd until just before midnight, and then silence descended on Ballinamore on the last day of service on the Cavan & Leitrim Railway.

4-4-0 No. 2 *Kathleen* takes water at Arigna on 24th September, 1934. It looks like a member of the station staff is assisting the engine crew with watering; the man standing atop the water tanks is smartly dressed in three piece suit with tie, white shirt and tails, hands on hip unruffled as No. 2 considers blowing off. [Photo:A.W. Croughton]

4-4-0T No. 2 *Kathleen* stands in the sunshine at Arigna on 24th September, 1934 with her safety valves feathering whilst the driver and guard look on. The driver's white shirt looks particularly pristine. [Photo: A.W. Croughton]

The first group of imported locomotives arrive in 1934. Former Cork, Blackrock & Passage Railway 2-4-2T No. 13L built by Neilson Reid in 1900 was the first to arrive on 2nd August. She poses for the photographer at Ballinamore on 27th July, 1936 with 'rods down' and front coupling hook 'up' with the train crew dutifuly watching Ron Jarvis as he presses the shutter for the time exposure on his plate glass camera. As expected from such technology, executed on a tripod, the image is pin sharp, save for the wisps of steam emanating from the cylinder drain cock. Ron would have double checked all these things as he set up his equipment for the camera; and well he might as he would only have had some half dozen plates to expose each day so nothing could be left to chance, not even the angle of the sun. No. 13 is spotlessly clean, even though her lining is careworn and she has a patch on her coal bunker. The 'L' was added to the locomotive's number to denote the Cavan & Leitrim Section of the Great Southern Railway [Photo: R.G. Jarvis]

Neilson Reid former CB&PR 2-4-2T No. 13L stands at Mohill with a short passenger train for Belturbet whilst the whole train crew watch the photographer and a hen scurries across in front of the train. As with all C&L stations, the main building was on the down platform.
[Photo: A.W. Croughton]

4-4-0 No. 2 at Ballinamore in July, 1955 now fitted with GSR standard style chimney. No. 2 as seen here is now a composite locomotive. In 1940, the frames and motion of No. 2 were combined with the superstructure and boiler of No. 7!

Irish Narrow Gauge Album

The 1.50pm train from Ballinamore to Arigna stands at Drumshambo on 27th May, 1954 with 4-4-0T No. 4L taking water.
[Photo: E.S. Russell]

In a condition very far removed from that when it arrived from the Cork, Blackrock & Passage Railway in 1934, 2-4-2T No.10L nears the end of its days rather unloved but still capable of a good turn of speed, as she is about to be pushed round by three men on the small turntable at Belturbet in August, 1957. [Photo: Peter Allen]

In August, 1957, former Tralee & Dingle No. 3T stands by Arigna colliery with seven wagons each loaded with the colliery's poor coal and each hardly looking as if they are actually on the rails due to their higgledy-piggledy stance. The driver is wiping his oil can whilst oiling up and checking round the engine. The guard is pinning down wagon brakes with a bar. Pat Whitehouse will chase the train down the parallel road all the way to Ballinamore, leaping out to take as many shots as possible in both black & white (using his trusty 1948 Rollieflex 2¼in square format camera) and the occasional colour slide (using a Contax 35 mm camera) when the train is stationary. The weather could be better, but photographers on long weekend trips from England cannot choose when there will never be another opportunity.

Chasing the train
All Photos: P.B. Whitehouse

3T 2-6-0T (re-lettered 3L on transfer to the Cavan & Leitrim Section) hurries the loaded coal train along the switchback route of the Arigna branch towards Ballinamore. Brake coach 5L and brake van have been added at the front of the train; however, the whole train is vacuum braked (at least in theory).

Former Tralee & Dingle Railway 3T (now 3L) hurries along the roadside with a mixed train of brake van and clerestory balconied passenger carriage followed by four cattle wagons. (And photo opposite).

3T arrives at Ballinamore station in August 1957 with a loaded coal train from Arigna. The line is fully signalled and the crossing keeper stands near his hut whilst the train rolls over the crossing while he waits to reopen the gates to the roadway. Even though the railway finances are parlous, the state railway, CIE continue to run it as part of their overall system with no concessions to the narrow gauge in the rule book at least. It has been raining. A girl parks her bicycle outside the shop behind the engine whilst her mother waits, also with her own bicycle.

Ballinamore
All Photos: Pat Whitehouse, August Bank Holiday, 1958

4-4-0T No. 2L stands outside Ballinamore shed amongst an array of wagon wheels.

A conversation piece by Kerr, Stuart 2-6-0T No. 4T with the local garage behind over the wall. The Kerr, Stuart locomotives were most unpopular when on the Tralee & Dingle Railway as their braking power was held to be inferior by the crews there, but No. 4T proved popular enough on the C&L having a larger cab than the Hunslets.

Coaling No. 3T on Ballinamore shed. The fireman is standing on top of the coal in a 5 ton wagon with the C.I.E 'snail' emblem on its side and the poor coal is flying off the shovel onto the cab floor.

Locomotives line up in a smoke screen on shed: a C&L 4-4-0T 3L stands out of steam on the left; the other two locomotives have been transferred from the Tralee & Dingle Section: Kerr, Stuart 2-6-0T No. 4T and Hunslet 2-6-0T No. 3T, the latter standing by the water tower whilst its fireman throws coal into the cab from a neighbouring wagon.

The unique Hunslet 2-6-2T No. 5T (transferred from the T&D) shunts in Ballinamore yard in August, 1958. This locomotive still survives. Having been exported to the USA by Edgar T. Mead for preservation, 5T was repatriated by dedicated Irishmen determined to revive a section of the Tralee & Dingle, which they duly succeeded in doing…for a while. [Photo: P.B. Whitehouse]

A short train headed by one of the line's 4-4-0Ts No.4L comprised only of a rebuilt coach and van stands in Ballinamore station in August, 1958. A family has just got down from the train. Everywhere is wet from recent rain. [Photo: P.B. Whitehouse]

Former C.B.&P. 2-4-2T now renumbered 13L, stands by the fine stone water tower at Dromod. [Photo: P.B. Whitehouse]

4-4-0T No. 4L arrives at Dromod with a short train from Ballinamore, formed of only a 4 wheeled van and rebodied carriage No. 7L

[Photo: Derek Cross]

Former T&D 2-6-0T No. 6T, now with its number just chalked on the buffer beam, stands billowing out smoke from the poor Arigna coal at Dromod waiting to depart for Ballinamore at 12.20pm on the last day of service on 31st March, 1959 described in the text. Inevitably the train was well patronised, especially by visiting enthusiasts from England and so the train had been strengthened to four coaches and two vans.
[Photo: P.J. Lynch]

The Light Railway Transport League organised several 'last trips' over the Irish narrow gauge. On 8th June, 1953 they chartered 4-4-0T No. 3L on a train to *Arigna*; possibly the first time ever (but certainly for a very long time) that a passenger train had ventured there. Here the train with the League's headboard pauses by the roadside for the *cognoscenti* of railway enthusiasts to photograph it. Locomotive crew and guard stand by the train and a horse and cart has been halted in the background so as not to interrupt the photographic activity.
[Photo: R.G. Jarvis]

Peter Allen took this photo and wrote on the back of the print: 'Two of the ingenious and compact works engines designed and built in Dublin for Guinness' brewery, to run on 1ft 10in gauge'. The engines shown are No's 24 & 15. [Photo: Peter Allen]

Chapter Seven

No. 12 resting in a converter wagon at St. James' Gate Brewery, Dublin. [Photo: Peter Allen]

Guinness Brewery

The Guinness Brewery in Dublin is justly famous for its product brewed with the waters of the River Liffey. It had an extraordinary railway run by ingenious and compact 1ft 10in steam locomotives designed by Samuel Geoghegan. From the early 19th century onwards, the brewery was a large concern and used a horse tramway to connect with the river. But in the middle of that century the brewery's output increased thirty fold, requiring the brewery to expand and modernise.

In 1872 Samuel Geoghegan joined the firm and by 1875 he was Head Engineer. He designed a new and improved narrow gauge network which could negotiate the existing buildings and move raw materials from the nearby Great Southern & Western Railway and its barges on the quay. It would also move the finished product back the same way for distribution. Geoghegan had to work within some constraints: the track gauge was set at 1ft 10in, the headway was only 6ft, the maximum width 5ft and the maximum gradient was to be no steeper than 1 in 40. This latter aspect clearly called for innovation as there was a difference in levels across the site of 60ft! Geoghegan dealt with this by using an ingenious spiral tunnel which raised the track 35ft and included a 1 in 39 gradient.

The railway was designed to move ingredients around the brewery in accordance with its 'flow line,' delivering empty barrels for washing, barley and hops to the hop stores and then onto the maltings. The railway then ran through the streets, with sidings diving off into granaries, malt and hop stores and then the maltings. From here, the malt and hops were taken to the brew houses, from where the spent grains were returned to the dock for dispatch as fertilizer. The wagons were side tipping skips together with open wagons for general stores and bogie flats for barrels and sacks. There was also a large flat wagon for the purposes of transporting the safe!

Geoghegan first tried a variety of commercially available steam locomotives but, as they generally proved incapable of the arduous operating conditions, clearly a bespoke design was needed. Whilst Geoghegan was a brewery engineer and not an expert in locomotives, he looked at the requirements with an open mind and designed his own engines having the best features of the earlier locomotives but not their problems. So he designed an 0-4-0 tank engine with horizontally mounted cylinders, above a marine boiler, which drove the wheels through a crankshaft and vertical connecting rods. The concept was to make the parts accessible for maintenance and repair and included a separate spring frame which could easily be removed for attention. Having the cylinders mounted on the top of the boiler (following fraction engine practice) made the locomotives easy and convenient to prepare for service. Avonside of Bristol finalised the design and built a prototype in 1882 also supplying as built drawings. Once the first locomotive had received some adjustments, Geoghegan instructed William Spence in Dublin to build 18 more between 1887 and 1921.

From 1888, broad gauge shunting was undertaken by these diminutive locomotives mounted in 'converter wagons' which they could be placed in and removed from by means of an hydraulic hoist. The wheels of the narrow gauge locomotive rested on rollers whose shafts were geared to the running wheels of the converter wagon at 3 to 1 reduction, so enabling a narrow gauge locomotive to become a broad gauge one!

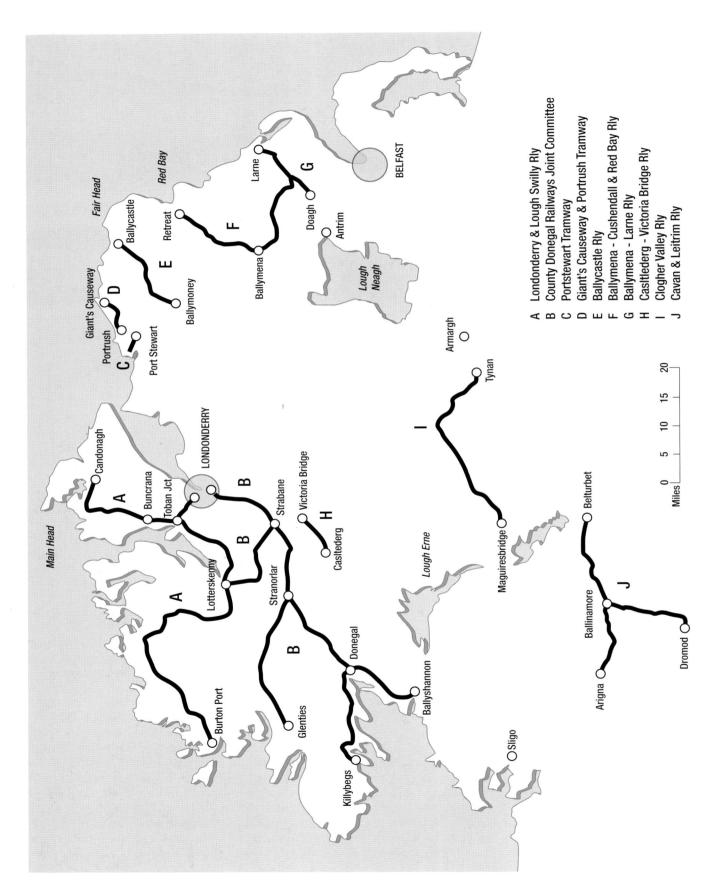

A	Londonderry & Lough Swilly Rly
B	County Donegal Railways Joint Committee
C	Portstewart Tramway
D	Giant's Causeway & Portrush Tramway
E	Ballycastle Rly
F	Ballymena – Cushendall & Red Bay Rly
G	Ballymena – Larne Rly
H	Casltlederg – Victoria Bridge Rly
I	Clogher Valley Rly
J	Cavan & Leitrim Rly

Narrow Gauge in Northern Ireland

NARROW GUAGE TRAIN .5185, W.L.

Ballymena, Cushendall and Red Bay Railway 0-4-2ST No. 60 at Ballymena with a train for Cushendall formed of two smart balconied bogie carriages and a brake van. [Photo: National Library, Dublin]

Ballymena & Larne Railway 2-4-0T No. 1 built by Beyer Peacock & Co. in 1877, Works No. 1687. This type was practically identical with the standard design adopted by the Isle of Man Railway. No. 1 features a leading pony truck with outside bearings, though the main frames were inside. The outside 11in. x 18in. cylinders were inclined at 1 in 9 and the slide valves had Allan straight link motion. The smokebox and valve chests were integral and the door of the smokebox sloped backwards. The original boiler was 2ft 10.75in. x 7ft 8.25in. with 103 tubes. The bell mouthed dome contained the Salter safety valves. The driving cab was formed by a wrap around plate which made the front, back and roof.

Chapter Eight

Narrow Gauge Compounds
By Pat Whitehouse

The year 1924 was a fateful one in north east Antrim for, during April, the Ballycastle Railway closed for the first time. It was the old story all over again – rising costs, some bus competition and the ever present problems of a small independent railway company since the end of the war; for independent the line was, though two of its seven directors came from the Northern Counties Committee. Fortunately for the local people, public opinion did not go altogether unheeded in those days and, after some altercation, the railway was taken over by the NCC in the following August. This body then carried out some rather drastic economies which do not concern us here, although the locomotive policy was of considerable interest, as the four engines left in use on the railway were in very poor shape. To fill this breach, three old

0-6-0 tanks were drafted in from the Ballymena & Larne section, while the two earlier Ballycastle engines were scrapped, and the other two, both Kitson 4-4-2 tanks, were brought to Belfast to undergo repairs and modifications with a view to their use on the Ballymena & Larne. Once these rebuilt engines reached that section, there was a transfer thence to the Ballycastle line of some of the Ballymena & Larne 2-4-2 tanks of Class 'S' and 'S1'. To appreciate the significance of this, it is necessary to go back some years to the beginning of the 1890s, when coal consumption figures were beginning to be studied by our railways and the compound engine was really coming into its own in Britain. At this time, Mr. Bowman Malcolm, who was Chief Mechanical Engineer of the Belfast & Northern Counties Railway, and constructed for that line

Ballymena & Larne Railway 0-6-0T No. 3 built by Beyer Peacock & Co. in 1899, works No. 1701. Seen here with an open backed cab as supplied. There were three of this type (No's 2, 3 and 6) all having inside frames and horizontal 13in. x 18in. cylinders driving on the middle axle. No's 2 and 3's boilers were 3ft 3in x 8ft (No. 6's was longer) and, at first, they carried brass domes with Salter valves (as shown here). The smokebox doors were hinged vertically. The three locomotives became 65, 66 and 67 in the BNCR stock list and, in the 1897 renumbering, 106, 107 and 108 of Class 'Q', all finding their way to the Ballycastle section.

Ballycastle station with a Class 'Q' Beyer Peacock 0-6-0T standing on the run round loop point for the engine shed road, a train in the platform and loaded wagons on the left. Behind and to the right of the engine shed were carriage and wagon facilities. Three such 'Q' Class locomotives were imported to the line from the Ballymena & Larne Railway by the NCC after takeover and renumbered 106, 107 and 108. Nos. 106 and 108 re-opened the Ballycastle line in 1924 and spent much, if not all, of their remaining lives working there, although the NCC was not averse to moving locomotives between their two lines, especially after overhauls and it is known that 107, at least, continued to spend time back at its original Ballymena & Larne Railway. By the time the locomotives were scrapped in 1933/4, they had accumulated some million miles each with annual mileages around 20,000.
[Photo: Locomotive & General
Railway Photographs]

several successful two cylinder compounds on the Worsdell-von Borries principle. He was a pioneer of compounding in Ireland and had cause to be satisfied with his experiments. Convinced by the performance of the main line engines, Mr Malcolm ordered the construction of two compound tank engines for the 3ft gauge lines under his control, the old Ballymena, Cushendall & Redbay and Ballymena & Larne sections. The engines were built by Messrs Beyer Peacock & Company (works numbers 3463–4) at a total cost of £2,060. They turned out to be strikingly handsome 2-4-2 side tank engines with outside cylinders 14.75in. by 20in. and 21in. by 20 in., the high pressure cylinder being on the left hand side. The valve gear was Walschaert's type and this was arranged so that both cylinders were linked up simultaneously. In starting, the high pressure steam was admitted to both cylinders but,

after the first stroke of the piston, high pressure steam was cut off from the low pressure cylinder and compound working began. This was the first time that compounding had been seen on the narrow gauge in the British Isles.

A further two locomotives were delivered in 1908 and 1909 respectively but, this time, from the York Road Works of the Belfast & Northern Counties Railway, which then became the only works in Ireland ever to construct 3ft gauge locomotives and the only one to build compounds. These engines were to the same design as their older sisters and were again classified 'S'; the cost was £1,679 each.

At the close of the 1914–18 war, some of the earlier narrow gauge engines in the Belfast & Northern Counties Railway's narrow gauge stock were becoming obsolete, so two further Class 'S' compounds were ordered in 1919 and 1920, both

being constructed at Belfast, the cost of £3,370 each showing how prices had risen since the days prior to the war. By 1920, a modification was made in the addition of a rear coal bunker, lengthening the wheelbase by 2ft and enabling the coal capacity to be increased to 1.5 tons. Engines thus modified were classed as 'S1'.

Over ten years elapsed before a further development occurred in 1931, when one of the original engines was rebuilt as a 2-4-4 tank, being the sole representative of this wheel arrangement in the British Isles. In this form the engine was never very successful, for the narrow gauge lines abounded in sharp curves and it proved to be too rigid in the wheelbase only running some 60,000 miles before being scrapped 1946. Of the other five compound engines, all remained until the closure of the Ulster Transport Authority's narrow gauge lines, with the exception of the last to be built, the 1919 engine, which was broken up in 1938, when narrow gauge receipts began to dwindle. The parts were used, in all probability, to keep the others running. They were pretty engines, these little 2-4-2 tanks, especially in

the inter-war years when painted in Midland red livery with the LMS coat of arms emblazoned on their cab side sheets. They really came into their own when the Ballymena & Larne closed to passengers, the unique narrow gauge corridor stock being transferred to the Ballycastle line. Three of them were kept on this branch, one as a regular engine, one as a banker on the Ballycastle to Capecastle section, which was severely curved and heavily graded, and one off for repairs. They were shedded at Ballycastle, but coaled at Ballymoney, where the operation was carried out with the assistance of wicker baskets, two of which were sometimes carried on the front running plate, giving the locomotive an out-of-this-world appearance. A journey behind one of these locomotives was the zenith of narrow gauge travelling, especially when riding in one of the really comfortable corridor coaches (even though the lavatories had been removed on transfer to the Ballycastle line!), for here were two complete novelties: the locomotive with its peculiar two beats per revolution of the driving wheels and the remarkable narrow gauge rolling stock behind it.

The caption written in the photographer's inimitable purple ink on the reverse of his print reads: '*Midland Railway (NCC) No. 105 2-4-0T (ex Ballymena & Larne Rly No. 4) at Larne 22.5.24*'. The locomotive is inside the shed apparently having some attention to its springs.
[Photo: A.W. Croughton]

The unique Ballymena & Larne Railway 2-6-0T No. 5 built by Beyer Peacock in 1880, works No. 1947. This locomotive formed the third of the BNCR classes and was itself classified 'R'. No. 5 was a tremendous puller and so was affectionately nicknamed 'The Bruiser' by footplate staff. It was not used between Ballymoney and Ballycastle but retained for use on the stiff bank out of Larne and on the Ballyboley to Doagh branch.

The first Beyer Peacock 2-4-0T No. 1, built in 1877, heads out of Ballymena with a short mixed train bound for Larne at the turn of the 20th century. Note the bracket signal with one post used for signal arms facing each way. The Belfast & Northern Counties Railway's broad gauge tracks to Belfast are in the foreground. [Photo: Locomotive & General Railway Photographs]

Doagh branch train consisting of a single braked coach and a van at Ballyboley Junction on 9th August, 1930 hauled by the lone Beyer Peacock built 2-6-0T No. 109. [Photo: H.C. Casserley]

Chapter Nine

The Boat Express, Ballymena & Larne Railway
By Pat Whitehouse

The railways in the north of Ireland had a character all of their own. They were earlier in the field than those in the south, largely due to the development of the iron ore industry, and they were more akin to the main line railway than to the roadside tramway more prevalent in Eire.

Of the lines which eventually came into the hands of the N.C.C or, in other words, the Midland Railway of England and its successors, the Ballymena & Larne represented two historic landmarks in narrow gauge history. It was the first 3ft gauge railway to carry passengers in Ireland and the only narrow gauge railway in the British Isles to operate a Boat Express composed of modern corridor stock.

Trains had run in connection with steamer sailings from as far back as 1880, when there were advertised excursions from Ballymena to the Stranraer Cattle Show for the modest sum of 6/9d return, first class and saloon, or 4/6d third class and steerage, but it was not until the twilight years of the passenger service that an attempt was made to provide a standard of comfort equal to the broad gauge. This took place in 1930 when three new carriages were constructed especially for this service at the Belfast Works of the NCC These were a complete departure from narrow gauge tradition, being of the vestibule central gangway type with lavatory accommodation, a previously unheard of luxury. There were two composite coaches, each having a seating capacity of 12 first and 31 third class passengers, and one brake third accommodating 24 third class passengers. Each coach was 50ft in length and 8ft in width over the mouldings, with bogie wheel bases of 5ft 6in. in length, the distance between bogie centres being 38ft and the weight 16 tons empty. The coaches were vacuum fitted

B&LR passenger train in charge of Beyer Peacock 2-4-0T No. 4 (built 1878, works No. 1828) at Larne Harbour Station. Whilst the photograph is undated, passenger services began in August, 1878 and this is clearly a publicity photograph taken when the railway was still new; for some reason the locomotive's smoke has been artificially added which has slightly spoiled the image of the chimney. The locomotive is exceptionally clean with the sun glinting off its burnished brasswork and posed with its rods down. Note the rods and crosshead have all been painted white. The locomotive was painted green and the carriages brown. Many years later, No. 4 spent some time on the Ballycastle section, then numbered 105 and classified 'P' and, subsequently, transferred again to the Castlederg & Victoria Bridge Tramway and allotted No. 6 and scrapped in 1933.

Bowman Malcolm, locomotive engineer of the Belfast & Northern Counties Railway and, later, the Midland (NCC) was a pioneer in compounding locomotives using the highly successful Wordsell von Borries principle. He designed a series of 2-4-2T compounds built initially by Beyer Peacock. The locomotive shown here, at Ballycastle on 29th July, 1935, is 2 cylinder compound modified Class 'S1' 2-4-2T No. 101 (with extended bunker added in July, 1928, resulting in the rear pony truck being modified so that the wheelbase was extended by 2ft). No. 101 was constructed in March, 1909, 16 years after the original class members and was built at York Road works. Originally numbered 113, she was renumbered 101 in February, 1920 and again as 41 in June, 1939. The locomotive was in service on the Ballycastle line numbered as both 101 and 41. She ran 469,761 miles in 41 years and was scrapped in January, 1950. She was a most efficient engine and popular with her crews. One claim to fame was a vigorous performance out of Ballycastle one day when a group of senior officers on a tour of inspection were running late and so asked for a good run to be sure of making their Belfast connection. The two coach train made the journey into Ballymoney in 30 minutes, which was 10 less than the schedule for the express timings between the wars and the trip left the Tow valley full of 41's echoes. [Photo: R.G. Jarvis]

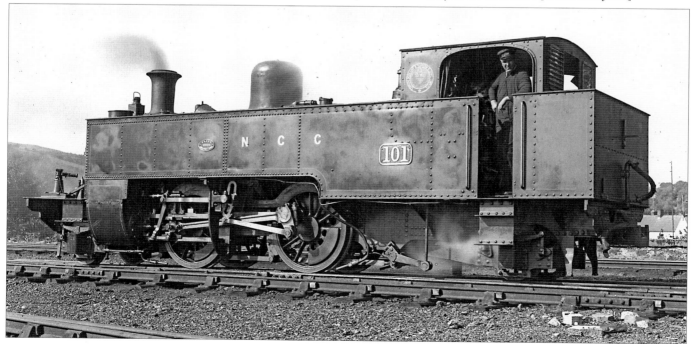

LMS, N.C.C 2-4-2T No. 111 on a short goods train at Ballymena on 20th March, 1939. This locomotive was one of the original pair of compounds to be built as No. 70, renumbered 111 in 1897 and further renumbered 44 in December, 1948. She was in service on the Ballycastle line for many years and ran a total of 1,156,774 miles in her lifetime. [Photo: R.G. Jarvis]

and steam heated throughout; electric lighting was by Stone's patent apparatus, the first class having reading lamps provided. The N.C.C were able to reduce some of the cost by using various standard fittings from broad gauge stock, but this does not imply cheesepairing, for they were magnificent vehicles.

The traveller to the west would have every chance of riding in this train, due to leave Larne Harbour Station at 9am each morning, for it was a definite connection and would be held up to 70 minutes for a tardy boat. The steamer was due to arrive at Larne at 8.55am, leaving very little margin for Londonderry passengers, if correct timings were to be observed, for the connection to Derry left Ballymena only 26 minutes after the scheduled narrow gauge arrival. Passengers joined the train at the Harbour, where broad and narrow gauge lines used the same station and where the clock was thoughtfully provided with two minute hands, one showing English and the other Irish time.

The journey time to Ballymena was one hour, including a stop at Kells at 9.49am, this being five miles distant from Ballymena. Punctual running was essential to maintain good connections and this was a particularly good performance over 25.25 miles of winding and heavily graded road. The first 6.5 miles were especially trying for, after a run of almost a mile on the level through Larne Town, there was a steady climb at 1 in 36 to Ballyboley Junction (7.75 miles) then up again to the summit, a further five miles, at 1 in 75. Here was Ballynashee, the Place of the Fairies, 650ft above the sea and well into the Antrim Mountains. From here, the running became comparatively easy, for the line dropped at 1 in 90 and 1 in 101, the last mile into Ballymena rising again at 1 in 60. The narrow gauge line ran alongside the 5ft 3in at the Junction station.

The return service left Ballymena at 5.47pm, this time taking one hour four minutes with additional stops at Ballyboley and

Narrow gauge double header leaving Ballycastle. A pair of compound 2-4-2Ts Nos. 101 and 102, built for the Ballymena & Larne Railway but transferred to the Ballycastle section by the L.M.S, head the 3.58pm train for Ballymoney, the junction with the Londonderry to Belfast main line, on 12th July, 1935. The carriages were also transferred, having originally been built by the L.M.S in 1928 for boat trains. Double heading usually occurred on the last train of the day during Lammas Fair occasions with the two engines taking all six carriages (which had formed the two sets during the day).

2-4-2T No. 44 on Ballycastle shed. Note her chimney has a patched sleeve fitted probably in an attempt to fix a crack.

Larne Town, with a call at Ballynashee on Saturdays. This was also a good performance in view of the number of stops involved.

The locomotives used on the Boat Trains were not of original Ballymena & Larne design, for they were imported from the 3ft gauge Ballycastle section, also NCC owned. There were two of them, both 4-4-2 tanks, built by Kitson's of Leeds in 1908. These engines were designed for speeds of up to 30 mph, but were not ideally suited to the work over this hilly road, for they were very liable to slip owing to insufficient weight on the driving wheels. As running on the Ballymena & Larne, the appearance of these engines was marred by cut down cabs and boiler mountings, the butchery being made necessary by the more restricted loading gauge of their adopted line.

The Boat Train services were the fastest runs on the Irish narrow gauge, but they proved to be short lived, for the end came during April, 1932. The following year, passenger services ceased altogether during a railway strike and were never resumed. The coaches were transferred to the Ballycastle branch to join a similar vehicle specially built for that line. When this closed in 1950, three were purchased by the County Donegal Railways Joint Committee, being used mainly for excursion services. They looked particularly fine in their red

and cream colours with the coat of arms of the company, the crest of the O'Donnell Clan, proudly displayed on their panelling.

The junction at Ballymena was not only with the broad gauge NCC main line from Belfast to Londonderry, but was also an end on junction with the earlier Ballymena-Cushendall & Red Bay. This line had pressed on as far as Retreat, through bare moorland country, right into the heart of the Antrim Mountains, attaining the altitutde of 1,045ft at Essathan Siding before descending steeply to Retreat at 1 in 37. The line was, for a great part of its length, close to the road and heavily graded at 1 in 60 or 1 in 52 and with no less than seven miles at 1 in 40, all against eastbound trains. The reason for the junction at Ballymena was that the iron ore mines about the Vale of Cushendall had provided the *raison d'être* of the line and the inconvenience of double handling the ore on to the broad gauge at Ballymena was considerable. With the connection between the two systems, it was possible to run the ore straight through to Larne Harbour for shipment. Fortunately, the gradients to Ballymena favoured the loaded trains, although there was, of course, the in 101 and 1 in 90 climb to Ballynashee on the Larne line.

The passenger service on the Red Bay line ran as far as

Parkmore, almost, that is, to the summit of the long 1 in 40 incline, the time being 50 minutes for the journey from Ballymena and 40 for the return journey. In the years after the First World War, the NCC ran attractive road and rail tours over this branch, an example being Ballymena to Parkmore by rail, coach from Parkmore through the Vale of Glenariff to Cushendall and then along the coast to Larne. The cost of this trip from Belfast was only 10 shillings. Passenger traffic on the Parkmore line was seasonal, for it gave access to a favourite part of the Antrim coast and the well known falls of Glenariff, but it was insufficient to maintain an economical service and as the iron ore traffic had dwindled to nothing, all services were withdrawn over a period beginning with the passenger trains in 1930.

Ballycastle Railway 2-4-2T No. 44 being coaled up at Ballymoney in June, 1949. One of the endearing features of the Ballycastle section during NCC days was the use of wicker baskets for storing and conveying coal. Steam coal was brought to Ballymoney by broad gauge and transferred to these wicker baskets. To coal the 'S' Class engines, the small bunker on the fireman's side was filled, the contents of two hampers piled against the boiler and then four more hampers were emptied on the footplate opposite the firebox doors, providing sufficient for the return journey.
[Photo: P.B. Whitehouse]

2-4-2T No. 44 stands in Ballymoney station in June, 1949 with a passenger train formed of two of the Boat Train carriages.
[Photo: P.B. Whitehouse]

One of the 2-4-2T 2 cylinder compounds stands in Ballycastle station with a short two coach train formed of two boat train carriages in May, 1949. It was often the practice for the locomotive to carry a couple of coal filled baskets on its extended front buffer beam. Here, the locomotive carries empty hampers having had their coal emptied to fuel the spare locomotive kept at Ballycastle. [Photo: P.B. Whitehouse]

One of the first two 'S' Class 2-4-2T built, No. 111. This locomotive carried three numbers during her life, just like her class mates, No's 70, 111 and 44.[Photo: M.D. England]

L.M.S, N.C.C 2-4-4T No. 110 Larne on 20th March, 1939. This locomotive was rebuilt from a 2-4-2T in 1931, renumbered from 69 to 110 and reclassified 'S2', but was never very successful in its rebuilt form as its wheelbase was too rigid for the line's sharp curves and they lacked adhesion. [Photo: R.G. Jarvis]

Boat train engine, 4-4-2T No. 113 at Larne on 21st March, 1939. One of two Ballycastle locomotives as rebuilt by the NCC in 1926/7 for use on the Ballymena & Larne line, though No. 113 returned to the Ballycastle section for a short while during the Second World War. Note the standard NCC style chimney, cut down boiler mountings and cab, necessary to enable the locomotives to clear the Ballymena & Larne bridges. Two of these locos were originally built by Kitsons in 1908 to the design of George Bradshaw costing £2,375 each and painted unlined dark green. They were simply enormous, weighing in at 39.5 tons, far more than anything which has previously operated on the Ballycastle line. They were delivered with both steam and vacuum brakes (the latter would have simply been ornamental on the unfitted trains of the Ballycastle line), but they must have been reliable enough and gave service until the NCC reorganisation of locomotives on both their 3ft gauge sections. These locomotives also lacked adhesion as, though almost 40 tons in weight, they only had 21 tons on the driving wheels and so were also notorious for slipping. [Photo: R.G. Jarvis]

N.C.C Ballymena & Larne section narrow gauge boat train headed by 4-4-2T No. 113 at Ballymena station in 1930 hauling three of the five new carriages built at York Road by the N.C.C specially for the service complete with corridor connections and lavatory accommodation. [Photo: Ulster Transport Authority]

In 1928, the L.M.S built a set of new carriages for the Ballymena to Larne boat train, a journey which took just one hour. The carriages were probably the most comfortable and modern ever built for an Irish narrow gauge railway (possibly also in the UK as a whole!) being fitted with steam heating, electric lighting, lavatories and corridor connections. Carriage livery was crimson lake with 3/8in yellow stripe and a 1/8in red line around all mouldings, except the ends where only the 1/8in red line was used. Sadly, these carriages were introduced at a time when passenger usage was declining and they only had five years service on the boat trains before being transferred to Ballymoney. No. 352 is one of this fleet being a brake 3rd. [Photo: Locomotive & General Railway Photographs]

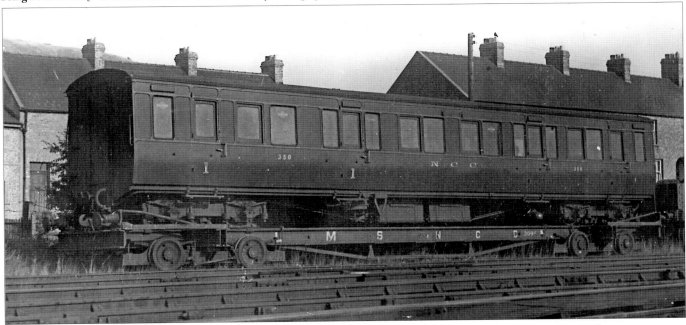

No. 350, boat train 1st/3rd when built, but converted into a 3rd class compartment carriage in 1936, the year this picture was taken.

[Photo: A.W. Croughton]

No. 41 compound 2-4-2T in Ulster Transport Authority livery at Ballycastle on 26th March, 1950. In UTA days, all narrow gauge locomotives were black, although No's 41 and 44 were enlivened by vermilion and yellow lining with the UTA's roundel in the centre of the tanks. The style of the numberplates retained B &NCR characteristics being cast in brass and of rectangular format. [Photo: J.I.C. Boyd]

Double headed 2-4-2Ts, both in the latter day UTA lined black livery, on a short two coach train about to leave Ballycastle.
[Photo: R. Ransome-Wallis]

Chapter Ten

Clogher Valley Railway

As we have seen, the narrow gauge railway came to Ireland largely as a result of English legislation. The first of these railways to be built was the Clogher Valley which ran from Tynan to Maguiresbridge in the North of Ireland. This was opened in 1887. A glance at the original prospectus showed the investor of the day that he was on to an obvious gold mine. The potential trade was painted in the most glowing of terms and the district was described as '*one of the richest and most peaceable agricultural districts of Ulster*'. As with most other narrow gauge railways in Ireland, the promised traffic never materialised. Not that the Clogher Valley was alone in issuing this type of prospectus – it most certainly was not.

The railway's name seemed to define the area; the Clogher Valley was not in common parlance before the railway came onto the scene. The area in question was in mid Ulster, mostly in County Tyrone but also in County Fermanagh. There had been all sorts of schemes for a railway in the area, but it was the passing of the Tramways Act of 1883 which provided the necessary process. After some debate, the final route was agreed and the capital required to build a line 37 miles long was calculated to be £150,000. James Barton, recently from the Castlederg & Victoria Bridge Tramway, was appointed engineer and a company incorporated in 1883. The Grand Juries of Tyrone and Fermanagh were convinced to provide the necessary guarantees and the Privy Council authorised

One of the steam tram 0-4-2Ts in the workshops at Aughnacloy on 19th July, 1933. [Photo: A.W. Croughton]

Sharp Stewart 0-4-2T tram engine, No. 3 *Blackwater*, built in 1886 standing in the yard at Aughnacloy pristine with a new coat of paint. The design has cylinders inclined on a 1 in 5 angle, possibly to clear the front driving axle. All of the running gear was covered by skirts as required in the Tramways Act to protect passing human and animal traffic. The class was rated at 70 tons maximum load on the railway's ruling gradient.

Three tram engines pose at Aughnacloy: Nos 6 *Erne*, 2 *Errigal* and 3 *Blackwater*. It looks like No. 6 has positioned the other two which are out of steam. The gentleman standing proudly between them may well be the manager. No. 3 is in her new coat of paint.

Aughnacloy engine shed with No. 2 *Errigal*, No. 3
Colebrooke and No. 7 *Blessingbourne*, the latter being
the solitary Hudswell Clarke 0-4-4T, all outside the
workshops.

the 3ft gauge line to proceed. But, almost immediately, the project ran into trouble: Salter and Sons, a finance house, who had agreed to underwrite up to £70,000 worth of shares if not taken by the public, reneged on the deal and the CVR almost became bankrupt before it had begun. The Board of Works were persuaded to make a loan of £44,000 which enabled the railway to be completed and opened for traffic in May, 1887, but already in debt before it had even taken its first fares.

Most of the tramway, for that is what it really was, followed the public road, save for the run from Fivemiletown to Maguiresbridge. The headquarters at Aughnacloy were quite over the top for such an undertaking: a large brick built station with two platforms for only two daily trains.

The tramway continued to fail to make a profit for the next seven years and, for the whole of its lifetime, it failed miserably to live up to the promises in its prospectus. Even in the best year, 1904, traffic receipts only produced £791

by way of surplus although the shareholders may have been surprised (perhaps overjoyed) to receive a dividend of £5,375. But never again, for example in the 1920s the annual deficit was always more than £7,000. Despite this, megalomania persisted with all sorts of expansion plans, even to meet the Cavan & Leitrim at Bawnboy Road, take over the railway and the Arigna coal mines. The name of the tramway was changed to Clogher Valley Railway to suit. Of course, nothing more materialised.

The CVR ordered six 0-4-2T tram engines from Sharp Stewart in 1885 and these ran until the line's closure, joined by an 0-4-4T built by Hudswell Clarke although this was not a success. The only other locomotive acquired was a second hand 2-6-0T bought from the Castlederg & Victoria Bridge Tramway and converted into a 2-6-2T in the railway's own workshops. In 1932, the railway moved into diesel motive power and this gradually became the

Fair exchange: Former Castlederg & Victoria Bridge Tramway Hudswell Clarke 2-6-0T No. 4, rebuilt as a 2-6-2T at Aughnacloy Works in 1936, having been exchanged for No. 7 and No. 1 *Caledon*. The locomotive heads a train standing at Aughnacloy station whilst receiving coal loaded into buckets by the crew and traversed over to the locomotive by means of the rails grouted into the water tower. [Photo: A.W. Croughton]

2-6-2T No. 4 and train at Aughnacloy on 13th May, 1937. The locomotive is lined out and beautifully clean and the locomotive crew are dutifully looking at the photographer from the cab. [Photo: R.G. Jarvis]

accepted norm for most of the traffic. First a rail tractor and then a railcar were acquired from Walkers of Wigan which then pretty much relegated steam haulage to the daily mixed running between Tynan and Fivemiletown. The railway also ran a steam tractor in 1928 built by Atkinson Walker powered by a vertical boilered geared steam locomotive; this proved to be useless and it was rebuilt with a bigger boiler but this did not much improve matters. However, as it had been supplied by the manufacturers on a trial basis and the CVR had not purchased it, its lack of suitability did not matter very much and so the machine simply stood out of use at Aughnacloy until the County Donegal bought it and rebuilt it as a diesel naming it *Phoenix* when it then started to be useful.

In 1922, the new Northern Irish Government set up a commission to look into the railways in the six counties which recommended that the Great Northern Railway of Ireland take over the line. But the GNR declined to do so and so the railway carried on with the ratepayers of Tyrone and Fermanagh continuing to subsidise it until, in 1927, a second enquiry recommended that the shareholders establish a Committee of Management to buy them out which duly occurred: the shareholders accepted an offer from the Government at £6 for each £10 share. Not that this process reversed the loss making trend though and so the railway eventually closed with the last train running on 31st December, 1941. The diesel tractor and the railcar were snapped up by the County Donegal Joint Committee as its manager, Henry Forbes, had already been convinced of their usefulness in containing costs on the CDRJC and, as he was also a member of the railway's Committee of Management, had the early chance to buy.

0-4-2T No. 6 *Erne* runs down the main street in Fivemiletown with her mixed train.

0-4-2T No. 2 *Errigal* and water tank wagon at Aughnacloy in July, 1933. [Photo: A.W. Croughton]

0-4-2T No. 6 *Erne* on the return journey stands at Clogher station with a mixed train.

0-4-2T No. 6 *Erne* on the 9.50am mixed from Maguiresbridge to Tynan at Fivemiletown on 19th July, 1933. Locomotives always hauled their trains bunker first to give the crew the best visibility of the road and adjacent railway on the tramway system. [Photo: A. W. Croughton]

0-4-2T No. 6 *Erne* on the 10.45am mixed train at Tynan ready to depart for the journey to Maguiresbridge on 13th July, 1935. By this date, this was the only remaining steam working on the line as the other trains had given way to being hauled either by the converted diesel lorry or the railcar. It is almost certain that the photographer and his colleagues (shown in the picture) travelled on this train and took the other pictures at stations down the line. Although the locomotive is clearly No. 6 which is *Erne*, the name on the side tank looks very like that of No. 4 *Fury* so it might just be possible that a side tank from No. 4 was used during a repair as No. 4 was dismantled for spares around 1925. [Photo: A.W. Croughton]

No's 6 *Erne* and 3 *Blackwater* stand at Aughnacloy with a very long mixed train. The occasion is unclear; maybe it is a market day train. No. 3 has been freshly repainted (as shown in earlier pictures) so it is possible the train might be some kind of test or trial.

The converted diesel tractor No. 2, built by Walkers of Wigan, stands at Fivemiletown with a short train comprising van No. 2 and carriage No. 15 on 12th May, 1937. Thirteen CVR carriages were made by Metropolitan Railway Carriage & Wagon Co. Ltd in 1887 with clerestory roofs and end balconies. When 1st class was abolished in 1928, all the 3rd class carriages were upgraded to have their wooden seats upholstered.
[Photo: R.G. Jarvis]

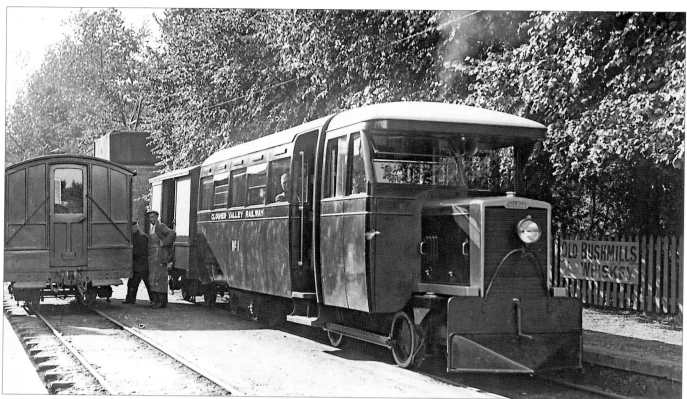

Walker railcar No. 1 stands in Aughnacloy station in July, 1933. On closure of the CVR, this railcar was purchased by the County Donegal where it became No. 10 and is now preserved at the Cultra Museum in Northern Ireland. [Photo: A.W. Croughton]

Aughnacloy station looking towards Ballygawley on 19th July, 1933. An enormous structure for the paucity of traffic. [Photo: A.W. Croughton]

Chapter Eleven

High Wind on the Owencarrow Viaduct
By Pat Whitehouse
[Extracted fom Narrow Gauge Album]

One of the wildest lines of all was the Burtonport Extension of the Londonderry and Lough Swilly Railway. It was built to the 3ft gauge with the intention of opening up the country, but it carefully avoided all the centres of population for, to go west, it had to encircle those great hills of Muckish and Errigal, often snow capped in the bitter winters of this part of Ireland. It was a difficult line to build, for bogs and treeless wastes are not friendly places, especially when western gales sweep down from the mountains; perhaps the most difficult section of all was the crossing of the Owencarrow Valley, for here the contractors met not only a bog but an almost bottomless one.

The Owencarrow Valley is part of the great rift which includes the Great Glen of Scotland from Inverness to Fort William; it crosses Donegal from the north east to the west coast where it runs out at the head of the Gweebarra estuary.

Londonderry & Burtonport Extension Railway No. 14, Hawthorn, Leslie & Co. 4-6-2T, built in 1910 at a cost of £2,050 and with works No. 2802, which hauled the train involved in the Owencarrow viaduct disaster. One of two built at the same time (the other being No. 13), these locomotives had a water capacity of 1,300 gallons, in an attempt to match that of the two tender engines, but they were unpopular with crew who held that they rolled badly at speed, probably as a result of having too high a centre of gravity. No. 14 was scrapped in 1943.

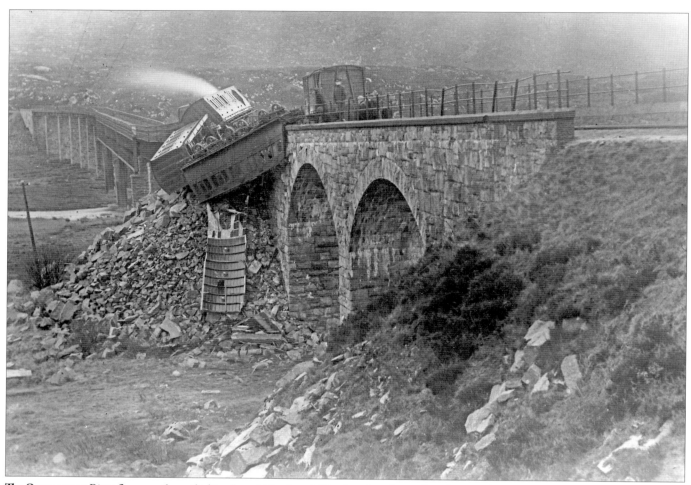

The Owencarrow River flows north east linking Lough Veagh and Glen Lough and its valley obstructed the path of the builders of the Londonderry & Burtonport Extension Railway, requiring them to build a long viaduct over the valley floor, curiously made up of girder spans, a short stone embankment and two masonry arches. The difficulty in crossing the valley was made worse by the necessity of a 1 in 50 fall from Barnes Gap and a 13 chain curve bringing the line round through a right angle and onto the approach embankment. The falling gradient persisted to the end of the tenth span, levelled out and then rose on a 1 in 50 gradient. Trains had been blown off the line before on this railway but by far the worst occasion was on 30th January, 1925. This view shows the structure and disposition of the viaduct with the wreckage of the train blown of the rails.

This shallow valley, which forms a funnel for the winds from the Atlantic, was crossed by the Burtonport Extension, on a viaduct of stone and steel 360 yards long and on an average forty feet high; its stone foundations went down 80ft through the bog before they found solid ground. The steel section of the viaduct was made up of 15 spans on masonry piers, it had parapets 5ft above rail level and there were strong wheel guards raised 2.5in above the level of the running rails extending for the whole length of the structure. The approach embankments also had parapet walls 20in thick and 18in above rail level. The whole was approached from either direction on steep falling gradients. The Board of Trade, unhappy but powerless, imposed a speed restriction of 10mph.

Now the men who worked out of Letterkenny and Burtonport were tough; they had to be, for the sleet, snow and driving rain of the Donegal winter were an integral part of their lives and the gales were accepted as a matter of course.

The passengers too were pretty hardy – again they needed to be, for the Lough Swilly, which worked the line, provided them only with wooden seated six wheelers plus the odd bogie coach, also with wooden seats. The best part of the bargain lay in the locomotives, running from 4-6-0 tanks through 4-6-2 tanks to some really massive 4-8-4 tanks and two tender 4-8-0s; these last two wheel arrangements never occurred in any other British railway. They could all do the job pretty well, especially as continuous brakes were the rule.

On 30th January, 1925, Bob McGuiness and John Hannigan, both of Burtonport, had No. 14, a 4-6-2 tank built by Hawthorn Leslie in 1910. Of all the Lough Swilly engines, No. 14 and its sister No. 13 were the least liked by the men for they reckoned they could be dangerous, as the water tanks were high and the engines rolled when running. The weather was bad, a storm had raged for most of the day and the outward journey to Letterkenny had been unpleasant,

Driver Bob McGuiness reported to the enquiry that: "*After travelling about 60 yards [over the viaduct] I again looked back and, seeing the side lights of the Guard's van, considered that everything was right. The wind was gusty and I was proceeding at the ordinary reduced speed and at the moment when I found it necessary to reach over to the regulator in order to maintain this speed I again cast another glance back, and then noticed that carriage No. 12 was off the line and raised in the air. I at once applied the full force of the brake and pulled up almost immediately. At that time, carriage No. 12 struck the wagon between it and the engine also sideways to the parapet.*" **Here we see six wheeled carriage No. 12, by then roofless, lying upside down on the Owencarrow viaduct after the train had stopped on 30th January, 1925.**

though no worse than many. No.14 had behaved well, the train brakes were good, and McGuiness who had been driving for 20 of his 25 years in the company's service, 13 of them on the Extension, was not unduly worried. He was used to it.

Coming back on the 5.15pm from Londonderry to Burtonport they had Neil Boyle as guard, and a mixed train made up of engine No. 14, a covered wagon, a six wheeled coach, an eight wheel bogie coach and a bogie brake van. The vacuum brake was in good order throughout with working blocks on all wheels except those on the covered wagon. The weather was rough but somehow it didn't seem quite as bad as the outward trip though they were five minutes down at Kilmacrenan, 5.5 miles from the Owencarrow Viaduct.

From Kilmacrenan they had to push their way down the 1 in 50 of the Barnes Gap for they were running into the teeth of the wind and, at the approach to the viaduct at around 8pm, Bob McGuiness slowed down to the regulation 10mph;

there was no point in taking chances. As they ran out over the embankment the comforting side lights of the guard's van showed clearly when the crew looked back and, as the gale was blowing hard, the driver gave No. 14 more steam; this seemed reasonable. Once they were over the last of the steel spans John Hannigan again looked back to see if all was well, when suddenly there was a particularly violent gust of wind (said later to be over 90mph) and, horror struck, he saw the first coach and the six wheeler, rise up behind the covered van immediately following the engine. He screamed over to the driver who also looked back just in time to see the coach blown right off the rails. Bob McGuinness stopped the train in a coach length but, by this time, the first coach was lying upside down on the embankment, and the other two were on their sides. Both men got down from the engine, which was still standing in spite of its reputation, and found that the covered van was also off the road, though it was still upright.

John Hannigan, then only 25 years of age, said to his driver: "*There is harm done tonight.*"

Although it seemed to the crew that the six wheeler immediately behind the van was the first to turn over, this was not actually the case. It was the second coach which had caught the full force of the gust of wind and left the track when its front end was 60ft from the end of the parapet of the steel section of the bridge; it had been dragged along the smooth surface without the enginemen or the guard knowing there was anything wrong with the train. As soon as this coach lost the support of the iron parapet, it fell over on its side but, before this happened, the six wheeler had reached the far embankment where there was no guard or parapet, and was blown off the rails in an almost upright position by the gust of wind rushing up the steep angle of the embankment. So strong was the wind, that this coach was lifted bodily off the rails. It was dragged its own length pressed hard against the lower masonry parapet above the stone arches, before it was completely blown over and held, in an upside down position, by its own couplings.

Four of the 14 passengers were killed and five others injured more or less seriously. Most of these were in the six wheeler which had its roof torn off, hurling its luckless occupants down over the embankment into the bog. That would not have been too bad had not a great pile of loose stones been dislodged and thrown down on top of the unfortunate passengers. One girl in particular had a miraculous escape; along with the others she was pitched out of the upturned coach, falling straight into the bog at the base of the embankment, though luckily feet first, sinking into the morass up to her knees. She was a local girl and ran home barefoot.

After this, the company ballasted all the carriages on the line, installed a wind gauge at Dunfanaghhy Road station and all the traffic was stopped when the wind velocity became dangerous to trains. The wind readings were regularly sent to the Air Ministry and, in January 1927, the gauge justified its existence by clocking up a gust of 112mph.

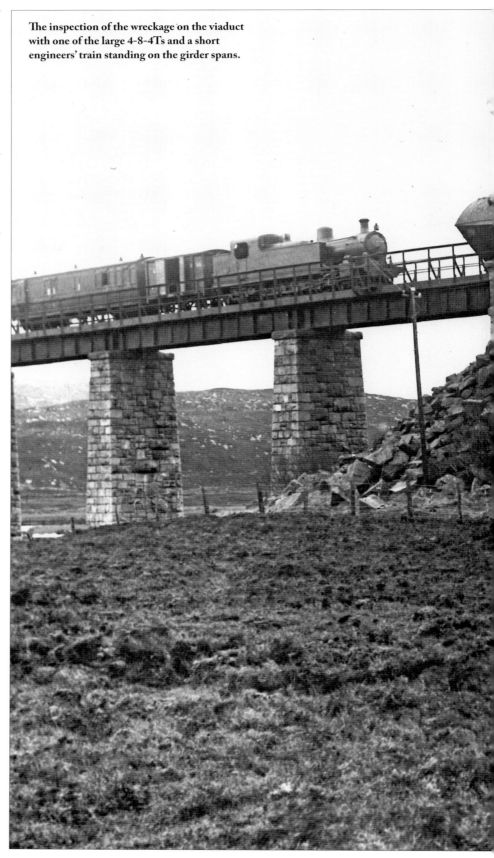

The inspection of the wreckage on the viaduct with one of the large 4-8-4Ts and a short engineers' train standing on the girder spans.

Pennyburn engine shed in the 1930s with the station on the right, Londonderry. This was the L&LSR's main locomotive shed and workshops. [Photo: A.W. Croughton]

A Round Trip into Eire:
Londonderry & Lough Swilly (& some CDRJC)
By S. Baillie Reynolds

It was snowing very hard, on 4th January, 1949, when I arose and made my way to the Londonderry & Lough Swilly running shed at Pennyburn, which is in Derry. I had an authority from the Locomotive Superintendent (W. Napier Esq.) to present to Driver Turner so that I could travel on the footplate by the 9.30am goods ex Derry to Letterkenny. It had to be a goods train because the Swilly suspends all passenger services during the winter months.

The engine was 4-6-2T No. 15, built in 1899 by Hudswell Clarke. The snow had temporarily ceased and we backed out onto the Strand Road level crossing. Being the first engine over the crossing that morning, and since the snow had been packed into ice by passing road vehicles, we came ignominiously to a standstill, driving wheels spinning furiously and uselessly. In our moment of impotence I could not but notice that, although the railway is only 3ft gauge, the interior of the engine is not

The locomotive footplated by S. Baillie Reynolds as recounted in the article: 4-6-2T No. 15, built in 1899 by Hudswell Clarke, seen here in June, 1949, the same year as the footplate journey, on Londonderry shed. [Photo: P.B. Whitehouse]

Hudswell Clarke 4-6-2T No. 15. One of two delivered in 1899, significantly larger than any locomotive running on the Lough Swilly ever before and the harbingers of what was to turn out to be the most impressive stud of narrow gauge locomotives in Ireland. Here we see No. 15 with some coal wagons. [Photo: P.B. Whitehouse]

very much smaller than the main line engines. A handful of gravel was enough to set us on our way again down to Swilly station. Like the other three termini in Londonderry it has two platforms and, also like them, has running behind it some of the three rail mixed gauge track which connects all four termini. The level crossing itself is single track and the opening of the gates works the signals direct. One of the signals is an ordinary semaphore, the other presents a red diamond at 'danger' and a green light at 'all clear,' thus the line is signalled to be 'all clear' regardless of the direction in which the train is travelling.

Having picked up an assortment of vehicles, including a bogie brake third composite, we departed, with no trouble on the crossing, for the border and the 80 minutes wait for the Eire customs. The distance is about four miles which we covered at a respectable 30-35mph. I cannot give any exact times for the journey since Driver Turner possessed the only watch and was the only one to know if we were late or early. We sat at the customs for 90 minutes waiting to do the shunting that was required there. Apparently no vehicles may be moved until after the custom's examination.

The snow would blow horizontally for some minutes and then cease for some time. The examination being over, we left

a van, picked up two more and then took water. Although I had taken several photographs I missed the most interesting – that of us signalled out onto a clear road with the level crossing gates still shut! The next stop was Burnfoot, where we left some parcels and picked up passengers; the use of the brake third was now apparent, for passengers may travel at their own risk by a goods train. The running was quite fast, with an estimated 45mph. I noticed that Turner never gave more than one third on the regulator, and that he did most of his driving on the valve gear. This method seems to give very good results. I was surprised that he never used more steam, for the track seemed quite good enough for higher speeds and, indeed, the riding in the cab compared very favourably with other journeys I have made at home.

We changed the staff at the junction where the Buncrana line goes off. The station has an island platform, signalled in both directions; the most remarkable feature is that at the junction end of the platform there is a combined starter for both platforms, the arm for platform 1 pointing the normal way and the arm for the other platform pointing the other way. The new staff was twice the length of the old and I was told that it was the Electric Train Staff. It was for the section "Junction-Newton Cunningham." We left the junction and

Three 0-6-2Ts with inside frames were ordered by McCrea & McFarland from Black, Hawthorn & Co. in 1882 and bought on hire purchase to work from Tooban to Letterkenny. The first locomotive was used by contractors to ballast the line, then becoming No. 1 *J.T.Macky*, named after the then chairman. Here we see No. 1 in 1900 at Buncrana on the shore of the lough from which the railway took its title. The train has arrived from Londonderry and some local lads are interested in the cameraman's antics. [Photo: Charles Friel collection]

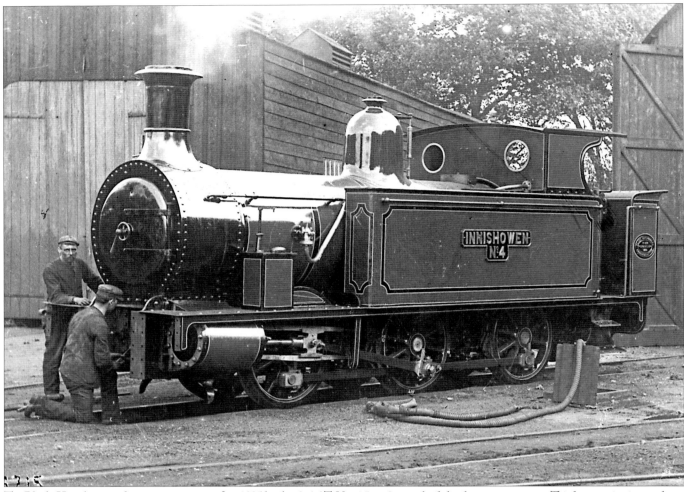

The Black, Hawthorn tank engines were joined in 1885 by this 0-6-0T, No. 4 *Innishowen*, built by the same company. This locomotive is seen here at Londonderry Pennyburn depot in 1900 still in its original condition with Salter type safety valves, an open backed cab and in its early lined 'grass green' livery lined black with and edging of white. She is having her valve chests attended to whilst the front buffer beam has been removed.

soon crossed a very impressive causeway across the southern end of Lough Swilly itself. Once across, we started to climb and descend gradients that varied so suddenly that I was the more impressed by the smooth riding and running of the engine.

The next stop was at a station whose name never appeared, but was remarkable for the ease and dexterity with which three bullocks were loaded. When we ran into Newton Cunningham, there was revealed the 4-8-4T, No. 5, which is, I hear, the largest narrow gauge engine in the British Isles. No. 5 had the usual brake third and also a carriage frame and match truck loaded with telegraph poles. It is remarkable that on a normal winter's day there should be four engines in steam to work a schedule that is purely goods, when the management has said that their railway is moribund. The engines are, as far as I could discover, stationed thus: one working ex Derry to Letterkenny, one working the other way, one working ex Buncrana to Derry and one working the other way. The Letterkenny train would naturally be the first to leave Derry as it is the longest run. We seemed to pick up an enormous amount of passengers, but I

never saw where they were put down.

No. 5 had left before us and we soon got underway again. At Sallyburn we stopped short of the station and uncoupled while the porter took the staff and unlocked the points. We then went forward, while the station staff pushed a van behind us; we backed the van onto our train and, after receiving the staff again (we had changed it at Newton Cunningham) ran on into the station. We then climbed up into a high valley and the hills closed around us into a pass. It seemed to me that at the other side of this pass there must be a town of some size, and that this should be Letterkenny. This proved to be correct. I put the question to the fireman that the Donegal Railway must come in round the other side of these hills. For answer, he pointed upwards, and there, descending on a slope appreciably steeper than the one we were descending, on the hillside, a good 150ft above us, was the Donegal. The sight was quite breathtaking. We climbed a short steep gradient and passed under the Donegal and ran beside it for a mile or so into Letterkenny.

Letterkenny is the terminus of three systems; the Donegal

No. 4 was renumbered as No. 17 in 1913 and given a taller and ugly dome and her safety valves were changed to Ramsbottom's design. She is seen here also at Pennyburn and in rather more worse for wear condition. Her rigid wheelbase of 11ft was found to be rather tight on the line's curves so the leading section of her side rods were removed for a while. She was scrapped in 1940.

No. 2 4-6-0T on Burtonport turntable on 1st August, 1935. A well liked class which survived until 1940. [Photo: R.G. Jarvis]

has a terminus of its own, with two tracks; the Londonderry and Lough Swilly shares a station with the Letterkenny and Burtonport Extension Railway. The latter is closed between Letterkenny and Burtonport and, to my knowledge, has no other track, although the line still exists for another 40 odd miles; it also possesses an engine on the Swilly in the original livery, and many trucks and vans, all of which have recently had the lettering renewed as 'LBER' In spite of this there seems to be no indication that the line will ever be re-opened. What LBER track I did see, outside the station going across the road and onto the west, seemed to be weed free.

I took my leave of driver Turner and his fireman, but remained to watch them turn their engine round on the turntable, which is too small to take the only tender engine – the only locomotive needing to be turned! Having ascertained that the Donegal train did not leave until 2.35pm, I withdrew into Letterkenny itself and had lunch. When I returned to Donegal station, I saw the 2-6-4T, which I had seen when we first entered the station, about to depart with 15 wagons and the ubiquitous bogie composite. The engine was manifestly smaller than the Swilly engine, and I cannot imagine it having an easy time up that extremely steep gradient out of the town. Allowing five tons per van, since some were heavily laden, and they carry seven tons with a tare weight of nearly four, and

guessing the composite to weigh eight tons, the whole train exclusive of the engine must have weighed 82 tons at least, no small load when the gradients to be encountered are so steep. There were no gradient posts visible which was a pity, since I can give no accurate guess at the steepness.

The railcar came in and I took my seat next to the driving compartment. It was an articulated car, with four coupled wheels driven by a Leyland engine. The car filled up very quickly and, at 2.35pm, we rolled slowly out of the station till we were clear, stopped, backed, came forward again, and then backed into the platform we had just left. About three minutes later we moved forward again and, getting clear of the station, reached top gear. The point of the backing was to pick up another carriage, but I cannot imagine why the extra carriage was not added before. As we left Letterkenny, I noticed at once the very steep super elevation on the exit curve from the station. I was to notice this again on the entry into Strabane. We made a good charge at the gradients but, as we crossed the Swilly, we changed down into third; at one stage I expected a change down to second, but the track levelled out. The snow which had started again in real earnest, seemed to make little or no difference to the running.

On this next part of the run, I saw little of interest, except that in two stations the passing loops had been torn up, but

Andrew Barclay 1902 built 4-6-0T No. 2 on a mixed train at Gweedore on 31st July, 1935. The goods trains also conveyed a coach in which passengers could travel if they were not in a hurry, as they would have to be patient at intermediate stations whilst shunting took place. [Photo: R.G. Jarvis]

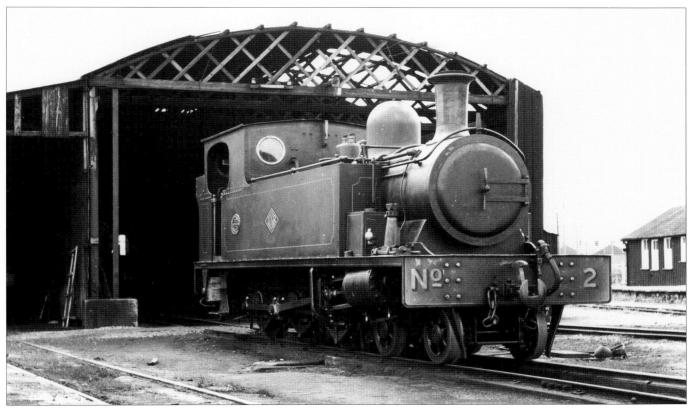

Andrew Barclay 4-6-0T No. 2 on Londonderry Pennyburn shed, 29th July, 1953. Reputedly the best engines on the system which gave a good account of themselves. They were designed by T.M. Batchen of the Irish Board of Works. [Photo: K.C. Cooper]

the platforms still remained. I dozed a bit here and so saw no other activity in the form of passing a train in the other direction, or anything else. We changed drivers at one point, stopping short of the station to do so. The next stop of any importance was the frontier station of Lifford, where the Eire customs people were very much in evidence; the British customs men are not so obvious when one gets back into the six counties. Lifford has one claim at least to railway fame in the shape of the bridge over the River Foyle, which is no mean feat of engineering. I should guess it to be a good quarter of a mile in length. It carries one track and, at the Lifford end, is of a tunnel construction. Towards the Strabane side, however, it becomes a normal girder type of bridge. Then follows the steeply banked curve into Strabane itself, which is the other side of the river, about a mile distant.

Strabane is remarkable, first of all for its name board, which reads, I believe, thus: 'STRABANE – change for Burtonport, Letterkenny, Donegal, Glenties, Omagh, Enniskillen and Derry.' Apart from the Burtonport bit, it is all perfectly true, and the LBER was open when the notice was first put up. It is also on the GNR (I) main line between Derry and Belfast. The County Donegal Joint Committee have a narrow gauge line running to Derry (Victoria Road), thus making Derry in the incredible position that one can take a train from any of the four termini trains leave from: the left bank going north, or from the right bank going south, and still end up at

Letterkenny; and trains leave from the right bank going north, and the left bank going south, and still end up at Belfast. The Joint Committee is run by the LMS (NCC) and from Strabane on is entirely Donegal. Where Strabane differs from Derry, Larne and other mixed gauge stations is that there is no three rail track. There is a short section of four rail, with the two narrow gauge rails well above the level of the 5ft 3in. to facilitate end on loading between flat trucks.

The point I made earlier about the size of the Swilly engines compared to those of the Donegal was emphasised by the presence of the 2-6-4T I had seen earlier at Letterkenny. It certainly seemed a lot smaller, but I have no comparative figures. There were two 4-4-0 tender engines of the GNR taking water before double heading the evening Derry-Belfast express to Omagh. This train had a Derry-Dublin coach on it. Since there was no Joint Committee train to Derry that night, I took the 6.5 pm non stop GNR train. Whilst waiting, I went into the GNR refreshment room on the Donegal platform where, furnished with a cup of tea, I sat by the very welcome fire; I noticed that, in accordance with it being the Donegal platform, the fender was made of flat bottomed rail.

Since it was really too dark to see anything, I slept in the very real comfort of a first class carriage all the way to Derry. I had covered some 60 miles of narrow gauge track, and 15 of Irish standard, in anything from nil visibility with driving snow, to clear sunshine where snow seemed out of place.

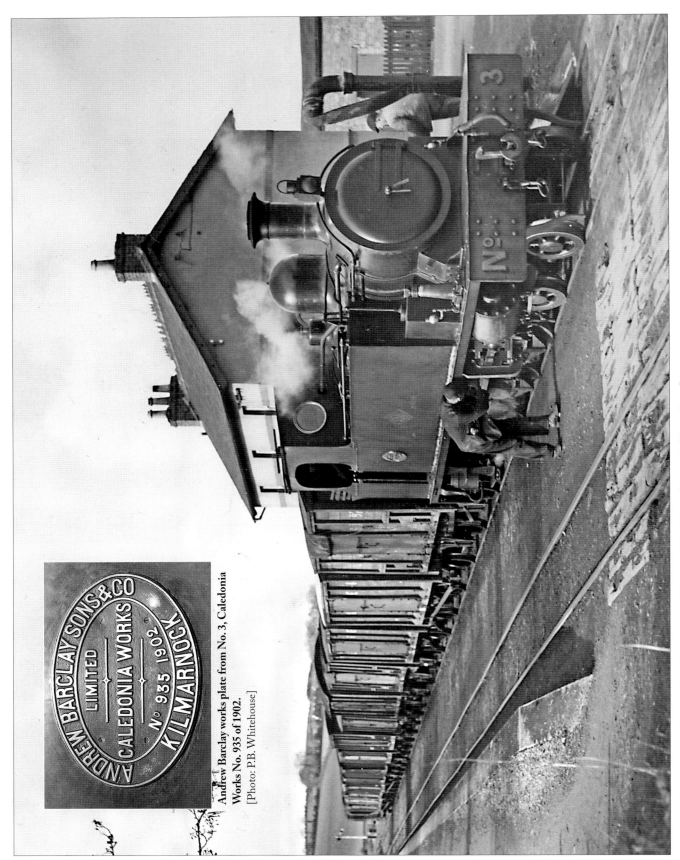

Andrew Barclay works plate from No. 3, Caledonia
Works No. 935 of 1902.
[Photo: P.B. Whitehouse]

Andrew Barclay 4-6-0T No. 3 on a goods train at Newton Cunningham station. [Photo: D. Trevor Rowe]

Kerr, Stuart 4-6-2T No. 10 on a mixed train at Newton Cunningham station on 13th July, 1931. No's 9 & 10, both from Kerr Stuart to the same design were referred to as the "Letterkenny engines" and were originally employed on the Londonderry-Letterkenny trains, for which their limited fuel capacity was no disadvantage. Originally named *Aberfoyle* and *Richmond* after the homes of directors in Londonderry, their names were later removed. No. 10 worked through until the closure of the line. [Photo: A.W. Croughton]

The 'Swilly' had a curiously inadequate terminal at the Londonderry graving dock where 4-6-2T No. 8 is seen shunting in May, 1937. [Photo: R.G. Jarvis]

Kerr Stuart 4-6-2T No. 10.

Londonderry Graving Dock station in 1933 with No. 5, one of the large 4-8-4Ts, most probably No. 5 shown in the picture below, being prepared before leaving. [Photo: A.W. Croughton]

Hudswell Clarke 4-8-4T No. 5 leaving Londonderry Graving Dock station with a well loaded passenger train in 1933. [Photo: A.W. Croughton]

Hudswell Clarke 4-8-4T No. 5, built in 1912, stands at Londonderry on 29th July, 1953. Two of these massive locomotives (No's 5 & 6) were built, each weighing in at 51 tons (possibly actually 53¾ tons) and with a tractive effort of 14,080lbs, the only 4-8-4Ts ever to run in the British Isles. Both lasted until the end of services in 1953 and solved the operating problems on the long Burtonport extension. They stood at almost 11ft high and 8ft wide; the fireman faced a difficult firebox over 8ft long; to avoid turning they were designed to run from Londonderry chimney first and return bunker leading; the build specification included a requirement for the valve setting to allow for either-direction running. [Photo: K.C. Cooper]

4-8-4T No. 6 with a Sunday excursion train at Buncrana in 1931.

Hudswell Clarke 4-8-4T No. 6 stands at Londonderry Pennyburn in August, 1947. Note the L &LSR monogram in the centre of the tank. [Photo: J.G. Dewing]

Beautifully clean Hudswell Clarke 4-8-4T No. 5 stands by the water tower on Londonderry Pennyburn shed on 27th March, 1948. The Hudswell Clarke records show a 'pea green' livery specified, with black & white lining finished with three coats of best engine copal varnish; buffer beams vermilion varnished with road numbers in 6in. gold letters (although the railway quickly asked for them to be yellow instead to economise); outside frames chocolate, lined red, with the inside frames vermillion. Quite a picture! [Photo: E.S. Russell]

Letterkenny & Burtonport Extension Railway 4-6-2T No.14, built by Hawthorn Leslie & Co. Ltd in 1910, seen outside the shed at Letterkenny. One of a pair, these engines were much bigger than previous engines of this wheel arrangement, but when transferred to the Burtonport line they worked turn and turn about with the 4-6-0s. The type was reported as 'very good, heavy on coal and water.' [Photo: A.W. Croughton]

4-6-2T No. 16 at Londonderry Pennyburn shed. When built in 1899, she was finished in 'pea green' livery lined in black and white and given four coats of copal varnish. With cylinders 15in. x 22in. she could develop a tractive effort of 14,050lbs.

L&LSR Hudswell Clarke 4-8-0 No. 12, works No. 747, built in 1905, one of a pair and the only narrow gauge tender engines in Ireland and the only tender engines of that wheel arrangement to run in the British Isles. They had Belpaire fireboxes and Walschaerts valve gear and weighed 37 tons but their wheel arrangement gave them a low axle loading of only 6 tons 12 cwt. They were bought in order to work the full double journey on the Extension without taking on coal. No. 12 worked on the Burtonport line until it was closed and hauled the demolition trains, then it was stored at Letterkenny for use on the lifting of that line and was then scrapped in 1954, just too early before any preservation thoughts could save her.

Hudswell Clarke 4-8-0 No. 12 at Kilmacrenan station. [Photo: A.W. Croughton]

Six wheel carriage No. 10. All the railway's carriages were latterly painted grey. Third class accommodation was rather austere, consisting of wooden seats, but the first class compartments were well upholstered and comfortable. Second class disappeared about 1930. There was no steam heating, but footwarmers were provided in winter to alleviate the long and rigorous journey to Burtonport, which was probably the last example of the use of such amenity once so common in the Victorian era. All carriages were fitted with automatic vacuum brake. [Photo: P.B. Whitehouse]

Londonderry station, June 1949 with a train of coal wagons and a brake third carriage. [Photo: P.B. Whitehouse]

Four wheeled wagons and one of only three bogie freight vans and a hand crane at Londonderry Graving Dock in June, 1949. Whilst those supplied to the Extension were separately lettered L&BER and built for the fish traffic, the wagons ran system wide. Van No. 45 is one of a total of 29 which had a centre canvas cover. [Photo: P.B. Whitehouse]

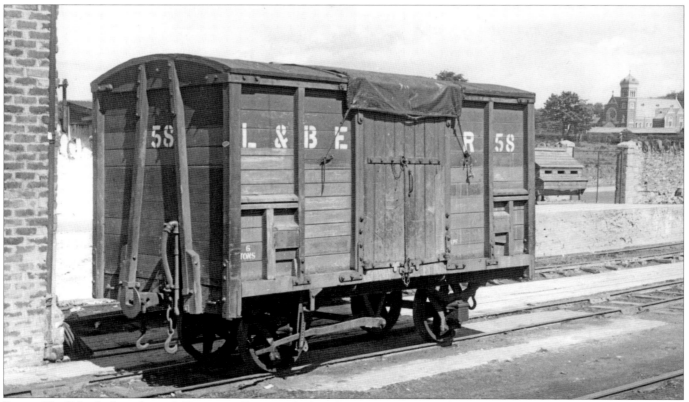

Box van No. 58 for the Letterkenny & Burtonport Extension Railway. [Photo: P.B. Whitehouse]

The L&LS turned to motor transport early. On 16th July, 1933 we see one of its then modern motor buses at Londonderry Pennyburn: a Vulcan Prince Reg. GE 5529, built in Southport, England, with a service bound for Moville, although the indicator blind may not have yet been changed when the picture was taken. Note the L&LSR over the destination blind. The railway began the transition to bus and road freight services in 1929. It closed its last railway line in July 1953, but continued to operate bus services under the name Lough Swilly Bus Company until April 2014, becoming the oldest railway company established in the Victorian era to continue trading as a commercial concern into the 21st century. Following a High Court petition by H.M. Revenue & Customs, the company went into liquidation and operated its final bus services on 19 April 2014. [Photo: A.W. Croughton]

The 'Swilly' also ran paddle steamers! Here is *Lake of Shadows* at Fahan on 16th July, 1933. Whilst Fahan pier was railway property, the steamers on the Lough were operated by several different companies ending up with Messrs McCrea & McFarland who formed the Lough Swilly Steamboat Company. They sold their company including this paddle steamer, built in Preston in 1904, to the L&LSR in 1923, for a total of £7,000. It was a brave move and never made the railway any money, although a lovely name for a steamboat! [Photo: A.W. Croughton]

Chapter Thirteen

The Donegal Railway
B J. Ferguson Walker
[Railway Magazine 1900]

The longest narrow gauge railway in the United Kingdom runs through a district of the most varied and interesting character. The Donegal Railway has not a long history, as it only dates from 1892 but, as it consists of an amalgamation of older lines, it is as well to go back to the year 1860, when the first of those lines was authorised.

At that time, the whistle of the locomotive had never been

heard in the wilds of Donegal. The nearest railway was the old Derry and Enniskillen Railway, which ran between those two towns and had connections with Belfast and Dublin by the lines of other companies. The natural outlet for the traffic of the greater part of County Donegal was at Strabane, a station on the Derry and Enniskillen Railway's system. There the winding and sluggish Finn unites the waters with the rapid

Essence of the Donegal (1): 4-6-4T No. 11 *Erne* shunts at Castlefinn on 22nd May, 1956. Frank McMenamin is on the engine.

Essence of the Donegal (2): Sunday excursions stand in Victoria Road station, Londonderry, on 29th June, 1939. 2-6-4Ts *Drumboe* and *Erne* side by side at the end of their platforms as their trains of red & cream carriages fill up with day trippers in readiness for the journey to connect with the NCC Portrush excursions. The somersault signal is 'off' to allow *Erne* to leave. Note the three cattle wagons behind; everything looks in good condition. [Photo: W.A. Camwell]

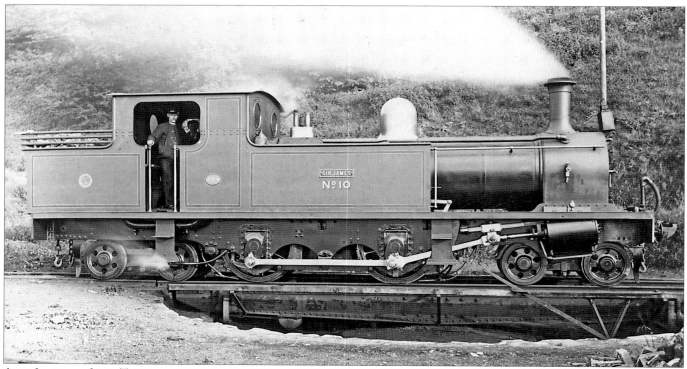

An early picture of 4-4-4T *Sir James*, No.10, built by Neilson Reid in 1902, works No. 6103, beautifully clean and with shining polished dome and safety valves; even the wheels and frames are immaculate.

and rippling Mourne to form the tidal River Foyle, whose broad expanse joins at Londonderry, the inlet which bears its name.

To and from Strabane trains of carts used to wend their way along the fertile valley of the Finn, and the road was enlivened by the rollicking drivers of Bianconi's 'long vans' and jaunting cars. The lie of the country concentrated this traffic in the Finn Valley as far as Stranorlar which, in those days, was a distributing centre for a vast tract of country to the north and west. Here then, was a district where a railway was needed, and where it could easily be constructed. The late Lord Lifford, a descendant of one of the Irish chancellors, saw the need, and determined that it should be supplied.

The situation of his mountain home, Meenglas, three miles from Stranorlar, inspired him with a local interest in the project; and his influence in England enabled him to assist the neighbouring landowners and merchants in raising the necessary capital.

Accordingly, an Act of Parliament was secured in 1860 for the incorporation of the Finn Valley Railway Company, and for the construction of a line from Strabane, 14 miles in length, and to the Irish standard gauge of 5ft 3in., generally known in Ireland as the broad gauge. Only one important piece of engineering work was needed, namely, the bridge over the River Finn at Clady, and as the Finn is a tidal river as far as Castlefinn, the Company was bound by the Act of Parliament to keep a light from sunrise to sunset on the Clady bridge for the navigation and safe guidance of vessels. Attempts

were made in later years to use Castlefinn as a port, and a stern wheeler ran for some time and for the conveyance of merchandise between Londonderry and Castlefinn. This had the effect of lowering the railway rates, and the vessel was appropriately nicknamed the 'Finn Valley Destruction'. The difficulties of navigation led, however, to the abandonment of the enterprise, as there was trouble with floods and ice in winter, and the water sometimes fell too low in summer.

The line was duly constructed, and on 7th September, 1863, it was opened by the late Earl of Carlisle, who was then Lord Lieutenant of Ireland. The day was typical of Donegal in the month of September. The sun shone in the intervals between the showers, and Lord Carlisle said in his speech on the occasion that he "*had seen the Finn Valley in smiles and tears*".

The new railway was a death blow to the business of driving passengers to and from the trains at Strabane, but the Ballybofey car drivers, not realising the positon, lowered their fares to a penny a mile and, nothing daunted, determined "*to run the Finn Valley off the road*". The attempt lasted just a week and, at the end of that time, the jarveys acknowledged their failure by ceasing to compete with the iron horse.

The late Lord Lifford was the first Chairman of the Company, and he held this post until his lamented death in 1887. No one took a keener interest in the prosperity of the line than he. No Chairman was ever held in greater respect and admiration by the servants of a Company. There once occurred an amusing incident in which he was supposed to play the principal part. The last train was slowly steaming out of Strabane on a market

Sir James, **near the end of its career, taking water at the Donegal Town engine shed water tower on 6th August, 1930. It was then being used on the Ballyshannon branch.** [Photo: H.C. Casserley]

night. She was already somewhat late, but the guard, leaning out of his window, saw a man rush across the rails, and heard him shout: "*Lord Lifford's coming! Lord Lifford's coming!*" The guard promptly stopped the train, and it was solemnly backed into the station to await his lordship. The man thereupon walked coolly up to a third class carriage, opened the door, stepped in, and putting his head through the window, called out: "*Lord Lifford's in!*"

During the early days of the Finn Valley Railway, the line was worked by the Irish North Western, which had swallowed up the old Derry and Enniskillen Railway. The Irish North Western was a struggling concern, and the locomotive they supplied was not of the highest class. It has been known to back the train out of Killygordon in order to get a rush at the incline on the other side of the station. In one well authenticated instance the operation had to be repeated three times before it was successful.

No further lines were constructed for many years, but Lord Lifford saw the desirability of railway communications being extended westwards from Stranorlar to Donegal and, in 1879, an Act was obtained incorporating the West Donegal Railway Company, and authorising it to construct a line 18 miles in length from Stranorlar to Donegal through the Gap or pass of Barnesmore. The difficulty of raising money for the construction of the line was great, for not only was the country generally in a very disturbed state, but the district between Stranorlar and the Gap of Barnesmore was sparsely populated, and was in fact chiefly moorland. West of the Gap the land

was more fertile and the population less scattered, but it was clear the line would have to depend mainly on through traffic between Stranorlar and the district west of the Gap.

The money necessary to construct the line as far as Druminin Station, now known as Lough Eske, four miles from Donegal, was eventually raised, and Lord Lifford had the satisfaction of seeing this section opened in 1884. This line was constructed on the Irish narrow gauge of three feet. It originally ended in a field four miles from anywhere, and it was popularly known as Lord Lifford's toy railway, it being the first narrow gauge railway constructed in the north of Ireland. All traffic had to be transshipped at Stranorlar. Lord Lifford did not live to see the opening of this line into the town of Donegal. This opening took place in 1889 and deprived the Donegal Carmen of the precarious livelihood they had earned by driving passengers to and from Druminin at 6d a head.

The autumn of 1890 witnessed an almost total failure of the potato crop in the west of Ireland, and the Government determined to construct certain railways, partly as relief works and partly with a view of permanently improving the condition of the people. One of the cardinal principles adopted in regard to these lines was that no line should be constructed unless an existing railway company undertook to work it. Donegal, being one of the most "distressful" counties in the "distressful" island, received a large share of the benefits conferred by the Government's railway schemes. Lines were constructed on the narrow gauge from Donegal to Killybegs, 19 miles, and from Stranorlar to Glenties, 24.5 miles, and were handed over to

4-6-0T No. 8 *Foyle* **stands on Donegal engine shed.** [Photo: A.W. Croughton]

4-6-0T No. 8 *Foyle* **stands at Strabane after withdrawal in 1937.** [Photo: R.G. Jarvis]

the Donegal Railway Company, which was formed in 1892 by the amalgamation of the Finn Valley and West Donegal Companies. The Killybegs line was opened in 1893, and the Glenties line two years later. The Company's system was now 75.5 miles in length, 14 being on the broad gauge.

The inconveniences of transshipment at Stranorlar at once began to be more acutely felt and, in 1893, an Act was obtained authorising the conversion of the Strabane and Stranorlar section to the narrow gauge. This enabled the Company to construct a short line giving them access to Strabane independently of the Great Northern Railway, which had swallowed up the Irish North Western, and over whose metals the Donegal Railway had hitherto been running for a short distance near Strabane. These changes were effected in July, 1894, all traffic being temporarily suspended for two days to admit of the change of gauge and henceforward the Donegal Company ran into their own station at Strabane, immediately alongside that of the Great Northern Railway.

The inconveniences of transshipment at Stranorlar were, however, as nothing compared with what they were immediately found to be at Strabane for, in addition to the goods coming from the original narrow gauge sections, all goods coming from the Finn Valley had to be transhipped, if they were going to a more distant point than Strabane. The same applied to goods going in the reverse direction and, as most of the traffic to and from the Donegal Company's system was with the port of Londonderry, 15 miles from Strabane, it was obvious that if the Donegal Railway could have independent access to this port a great advantage would be secured. They accordingly brought forward a scheme for a narrow gauge railway, 14 miles in length, from Strabane to Londonderry, to be built on the right bank of the Foyle, and they promoted a Bill in Parliament for this purpose.

It was a bold experiment for a small company to make, for they met with strenuous opposition from the Great Northern. The latter company's line between Strabane and Londonderry is, however, on the left bank of the river, and there is no bridge or ferry service at any point on the way. The scheme passed the trying ordeal of two Parliamentary Committees on 1896, and the line is expected to be opened in May 1900.

In the same Bill a scheme was included for a narrow gauge line, 15.5 miles long, from Donegal to Ballyshannon and this line, which was likewise authorised, will be commenced as soon as the other has been completed. These extensions will bring the system up to a total length of 105 miles.

From Strabane to Stranorlar the line runs through a very fertile valley, very unlike the popular idea of what County Donegal is like. At Stranorlar one has the first real glimpse of the wild mountains and lovely valleys, of which the greater part of the country is composed. Isaac Butt, who was the leader of the Home Rule party before Purnell, lies buried in Stranorlar churchyard. On leaving Stranorlar, the line to Donegal and Killybegs turns sharply to the left, while that towards Finntown and Glenties keep straight on up the valley,

The quartet of Class 4 4-6-4 'Baltic' tanks built by Nasmyth Wilson in 1904:

No. 9 *Eske.*

No. 10 *Owenea*. [Photo: R.G. Jarvis]

No. 15 *Mourne* in July, 1931. [Photo: A.W. Croughton]

No. 14 *Erne*. This was the longest lasting of the quartet, surviving until 1967 when it was cut up at Stranorlar; a great loss to history.
[Photo: R.G. Jarvis]

this part of which is known as Glenfin. After passing Lough Finn, where the river takes its rise, the line rapidly descends the moorland slope into the town of Glenties.

If we follow the direction of the line to Donegal, we notice at once a remarkable change in the aspect of the country. A long uphill climb brings the train to the summit of what is locally known as the five mile hill. To attain this elevation, the train, dragged by a little 'coffee pot' of an engine, slowly progresses over and around a series of bleak, half cultivated hills. From the summit the line is nearly parallel to the old mail car road, until both have emerged on the western side of the Gap of Barnesmore. Near the summit, and close alongside the railway, lies Lough Mourne, a long narrow sheet of water, harbouring pike which, according to local tradition, are of monster size. About opposite the middle of the lake at the side of the road, stands the 'Lough House', where, in the olden days, horses were changed on the journey by mail car from Derry to Sligo.

From the summit down into the Gap the train bowls along at a considerable rate, through a dreary waste of bog and across streams tumbling merrily to the sea. On the right may be seen a hill overlooking the road and marked 'Fort' in the Ordnance Survey maps. There, a garrison of soldiers was formerly stationed to convoy travellers through the Gap, which was infested by robbers. At an earlier period no such protection was afforded, and many are the tales of adventures formerly met with in these lonely wilds.

A good story is told of the way in which Mike Flaherty, a half witted servant from Ballyshannon, once got the better of Rory O'Hanlon, the chief of one of these robber bands. Rory rode a splendid horse, and it was generally considered hopeless to escape from his clutches. Mike's master was a trader in Ballyshannon, and wished to send to Londonderry for money. The only practical route was the dangerous one through the Gap of Barnesmore. Mike offered to go if his master would provide him with the worst horse to be found in Balyshannon. The master was skeptical. It seemed madness to send a half witted being, especially on a steed of such a character. Confident, however, in the man's loyalty, and thinking that the fellow might possibly have in his mind some feasible plan that would not occur to a wiser head, he determined to take the risk and despatched Mike on the most wretched 'crock' that the neighbourhood could supply.

On the way to Derry, Mike met Rory O'Hanlon in the Gap, entered into conversation with him, and mentioned that he would be returning to Derry in a couple of days with money for his master. In Derry, Mike instructed the banker to put £5 worth of coppers in one bag and all the gold in another. The banker complied with the request and Mike, full of confidence, set out on his return journey. At the entrance to the Gap, Rory, astride an excellent horse, awaited his coming. They rode along side by side for some distance and conversed on everything but the one subject of which each was thinking. At last, Rory told his companion that he might as well give up the money at once. "*Well,*" Said Mike, "*I must at least give you a bit of a*

run for it. It would hardly do for me to submit too readily." With these words he threw the heavy bag of coppers from him with all his strength. The robber immediately dismounted and proceeded to pick up the bag. Mike however was too quick for him. Throwing himself from his horse, he leapt into the robber's saddle and rode off at full speed. On examining the contents of the bag, a moment's reflection convinced Rory that the situation was hopeless. He had been outwitted for once.

As the train advances towards the Gap, the traveller obtains a magnificent view. An irregular chain of mountains stretches away to the north and south, with a narrow pass breaking their continuity and revealing a glimpse of the fertile country beyond. In the Gap itself the train runs along the side of the mountain at a height sufficient to give the traveller a commanding view of the valley below. Down at the bottom runs the Barnes river and, close to it, a road with a beautiful surface, now seldom traversed by any traffic except the ubiquitous cyclist. At a slightly higher level on the north side of the pass may be seen the track of the old road, long since overgrown with grass. About half way through the Gap there is a rectangular enclosure containing numerous stumps of fir trees - all that remains of what once was a considerable plantation. The story goes that a Trinity College student, driving through the Gap in an Irish car, carelessly threw a match into the enclosure after lighting his pipe and the trees were unfortunately burnt.

The train frequently stops to take in water from a waterfall coming down the mountain side. Just opposite may be seen a solitary building. This is a public house belonging to 'Biddy of the Gap', a regular character in her way. Many mountain tarns, filled with trout, lie concealed in nooks and crannies among the mountains on each side of the Gap, but none of them equal in size or beauty the lake which bursts upon the view shortly after the train emerges from the pass. Lough Eske, studded with islands and sheltered by trees, lies encircled by mountains to the north and east, and smiling landscape to the south and west, with the castle nestling in the wood close to the edge of the water, in which the dark background is reflected with striking clearness. Nearby is the cottage where the poetess, Frances Browne, daughter of a village postmaster, was born in 1816. In the lake there are many salmon and trout, including the species known to scientists as the *salmon ferox*. Lord Zetland, when Lord Lieutenant of Ireland, caught one of the latter and a local paper calmly informed its readers that he had landed a "*ferocious salmon*".

The town of Donegal boasts the ruins of an ancient abbey, founded in the 15th century by the Lady Finola, daughter of the O'Connor family and wife of Hugh Roe O'Donnel, chief of Tirconnell. For many years it was a centre of religious education, but in 1601 it was seized by the English and destroyed by gunpowder.

From Donegal to Killybegs the line is of a switchback character, owing to the severity of the gradients. The first station is at Kilymard, where there is a spa, which is said to resemble the springs of Harrogate. Between Donegal and Mountcharles the traveller obtains a splendid view of Donegal Bay, with its background of mountains belonging to the four counties of Donegal, Fermanagh, Leitrim and Sligo.

Killybegs, the terminus, is a picturesque village and boasts one of the safest harbours on the western seaboard. Vessels of heavy tonnage can come in at any state of the tide, and the Government has built a pier of ironwood for their accommodation. The inhabitants have even dreamed of their remote village becoming at some future date the rival of Moville in the north and Queenstown in the south as a transatlantic port of call.

Class '5', 2-6-4T No. 17 *Glenties*, built by Nasmyth Wilson in 1907, works No. 829. [Photo: R.G. Jarvis]

Class '5a', 2-6-4T No.3 *Lydia*. Built in 1912 by Nasmyth Wilson, works No. 957. The '5a' class were quite sophisticated locomotives, being fitted from new with superheaters, mechanical lubricators and speed recorders. [Photo: R.G. Jarvis]

Irish Narrow Gauge Album

Class '4' 4-6-4T No. 10 *Owenea* leaves Strabane Junction with a passenger train. [Photo: R.G. Jarvis]

184

Class '5a' 2-6-4T *Lydia* stands bunker first at Killybegs station with a train for Donegal and Stranorlar in July, 1931. Note the lovely ornate wooden overall station roof which was provided to offer passengers additional protection on the exposed harbourside location. Killybegs was one of Ireland's most important Atlantic coast fishing ports; behind the station can be seen the goods shed. There was also a line down to the pier for delivering oil to the fishing fleet. Rails still exist on the pier; the only ones on the railway still in situ. [Photo: A.W. Croughton]

Class '5' 2-6-4T No. 16 *Donegal* at Strabane station with a mixed train in July, 1931. Note the lagged water column to prevent freezing pipes in winter. [Photo: A.W. Croughton]

Class '5a' 2-6-4T No. 2 *Blanche* stands on shed behind piles of ash at Strabane in July, 1931. [Photo: A.W. Croughton]

Class '5a' 2-6-4T No. 3 *Lydia* in July 1931, at the west end of Stranorlar station with a train heading towards Donegal. **The building on the left is the company offices, the large building on the right is a store and the wooden building was used for carriages.** [Photo: A.W. Croughton]

2-6-4T No. 19 *Letterkenny* approaches Lough Mourne as it ascends to Barnesmore Gap on 30th June, 1939 with the 3.50pm. Stranorlar-Donegal & Killybegs goods. Railcar No. 14 is at the end of the train being hauled backwards out of gear and with the engine switched off in order to provide additional accommodation. All CDJR goods trains included a brake carriage as the railway had no brake vans; the one at the head of the train is No. 28. [Photo: W.A. Camwell]

2-6-4T _Drumboe_ heads a train of vans running through Strabane station in August, 1957. [Photo: P.C. Allen]

Class '5a' 2-6-4T No. 2 _Blanche_ waits bunker first with an excursion train at Donegal in August, 1957. Local kids are already leaning far out of the carriage windows anticipating departure time. [Photo: P.C. Allen]

Class '5a' 2-6-4T No. 2 *Blanche* heads into the falling evening shadows and begins the climb up from Lough Eske on a return Sunday excursion from Rossnowlagh on 3rd August, 1959, the very last bank holiday steam train on the Donegal. [Photo: P.B. Whitehouse]

Class '5a' 2-6-4T No. 2 *Blanche* stands with a short two coach train in the Londonderry NCC station at Victoria Road. The branch from Victoria Road to Strabane was the property of the Midland Railway (later the NCC) and the CDRJC were paid to work it. To the far right, the covered ramp which led up to the street. The tank wagons were used to convey fuel oil from Londonderry to Killybegs for use by the fishing fleet there. [Photo: P.B. Whitehouse]

Above and opposite: Even the railcars needed steam assistance in times of stress. Here we see Class '5a' 2-6-4T No. 2 *Blanche* coming to the rescue hauling Railcar No. 15 with the 2.35pm service to Letterkenny on August Bank Holiday Monday in 1959. Railcar No. 15 was the worst performer on the system and known as the 'black sheep'. In the first scene, the 'train' is standing in Strabane station. Note the advert for one of Ireland's best known products on the wall of the station building. On the other side was the busy station buffet. In the next shot, the train is leaving, now with a van added behind the railcar, as *Blanche* pulls past the signal box and lower quadrant semaphore signal en route to Letterkenny. [Photo: P.B. Whitehouse]

Class '4' 4-6-4T No. 11 *Erne* leaves Strabane station with a goods train, a 3rd brake coach bringing up the rear carrying the guard and maybe some hardy passengers.
[Photo: P.B. Whitehouse]

Class '5a' 2-6-4T No. 2 *Blanche* taking water at Ballyshannon. [Photo: P.B. Whitehouse]

Class '4' 4-6-4T No. 11 *Erne* brings the morning goods under the road bridge and into Killygordon, nicely identified by the freshly white painted stones setting out the station name under the bushes. In the post war years steam was reserved for the heavier goods trains and summer passenger train specials. [Photo: P.B. Whitehouse]

Excursion train at Stranorlar. This was the headquarters for the CDRJC and had a fine station building, seen in the background. The station was the hub for the system and junction for the one time branch to Glenties. Here were the locomotive works and carriage repair depot, as well as the main offices. [Photo: P.B. Whitehouse]

Steam at Ballyshannon. 2-6-4T *Blanche* making up its train for a return excursion to Stranorlar and Strabane on an August Sunday in 1952. [Photo: P.B. Whitehouse]

Class '4' 4-6-4T No. 11 *Erne* stands at Castlefinn on 22nd May, 1956 with a Strabane bound mixed whilst waiting the pleasure of the Irish Republic customs officers, as vans were sealed here; the line crossed into the six counties just beyond Clady, the border being the River Finn. One of the difficulties besetting both the Donegal and Lough Swilly lines was the Irish border. Even with efficient handlings and inspections this meant delays and thoughtless or rash passengers could cause delays of many minutes. What was worse, the towns and villages west of Strabane were virtually cut off from their old supply point at Londonderry and so began to trade with the nearest large town in the Republic at Sligo, by road, and this did not improve the freight traffic for the railways. [Photo: P.B. Whitehouse]

Irish Republic customs officer Alex Flood checks the wagon seals on a Donegal Railway van after examination at Castlefinn station on 22nd May, 1956. The train was then sent through to Strabane where the seals, which had an Irish harp on them, were checked and then opened in the transshipment shed. [Photo: P.B. Whitehouse]

The very last steam passenger excursion of them all on 3rd August, 1959, Bank Holiday Monday. 2-6-4T *Meenglas* climbs up through Barnesmore Gap in the early evening on its way from Ballyshannon to Strabane. The McMenamin brothers on the footplate get to grips with the 1 in 60 grade; for the next three miles, one of the most spectacular and dramatic of any Irish railway with the line clinging to slopes high above the road and river. Many passengers are leaning far out of the windows of the train waving to the photographers and others standing on the road, all entering into the spirit of the occasion. [Photo: P.B. Whitehouse]

Irish Narrow Gauge Album

A young lad watches the fireman prepare the fire at Ballyshannon as fresh black smoke comes out of the chimney of Class '5a' 2-6-4T No. 2 *Blanche* as she hauls the last passenger excursion train from Strabane on the morning of August Bank Holiday Monday 3rd August, 1959. Note the steel rod attached to the coupling on the rear bunker; this was used to keep the locking arm up when loose shunting wagons, otherwise the wagon would automatically couple up to the locomotive. [Photo: P.B. Whitehouse]

The McMenamin brothers, Frank and Jim, in the cab of 2-6-4T No. 4 *Meenglas*. At the end, these two brothers were the only Stranorlar steam crew left and so they took turn and turn about on the regulator and also firing. Old Frank was put off driving towards the end as he did not pass the medical, but even so the two brothers continued to work as of old, Jim driving the engine through Stranorlar, just in case someone was watching and, once out of sight, they went back to their former jobs. When trains ceased at the end of 1959, Frank left the service but Jim was kept on as a lorry loader, although he said it would never be the same again. [Photo: E.M. Patterson]

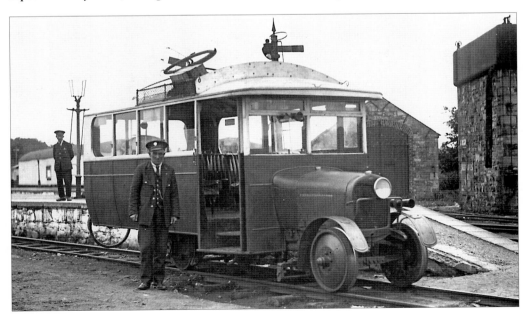

One of the ex Derwent Valley railcars, No. 4, purchased from the railway near York as a Ford lorry chassis and fitted with a sister vehicle to run back to back, using one of the motors at a time. Both were purchased by Forbes for £480. The vehicles were converted to narrow gauge by the Great Northern (Ireland) Railway at its Dundalk works. At Castlefinn, the Free State customs officers lay in wait and, in spite of protests, obtained a 33 ⅓ per cent duty claiming that they were motor buses. Here we see the railcar standing in Donegal Town station on 15th July, 1931. Note the bicycle 'thrown' up on the roof luggage rack. [Photo: A.W. Croughton]

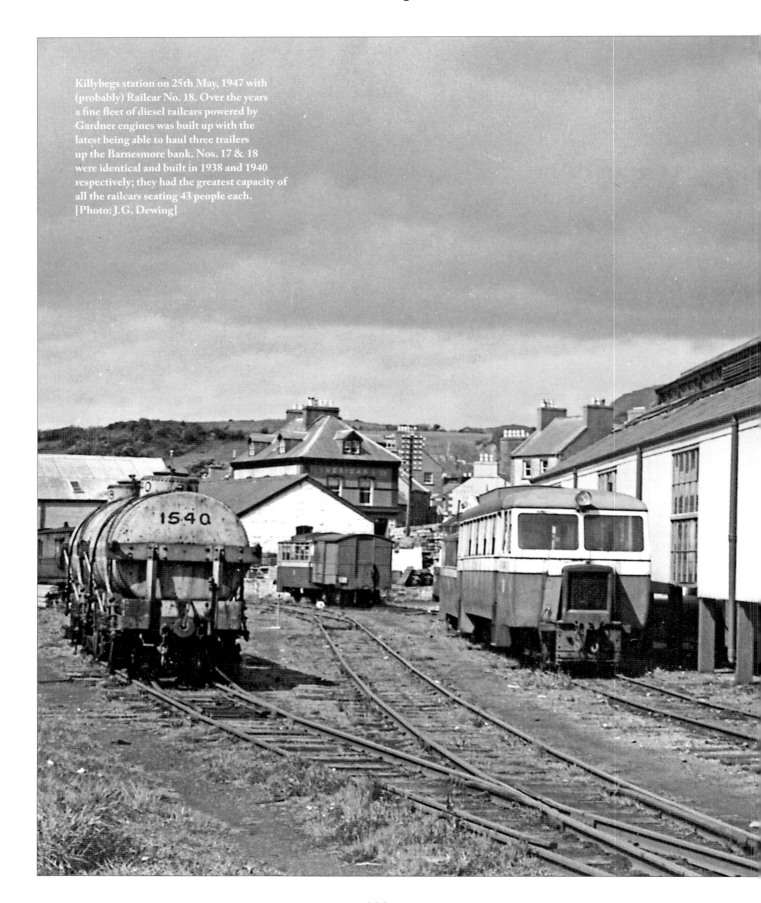

Killybegs station on 25th May, 1947 with
(probably) Railcar No. 18. Over the years
a fine fleet of diesel railcars powered by
Gardner engines was built up with the
latest being able to haul three trailers
up the Barnesmore bank. Nos. 17 & 18
were identical and built in 1938 and 1940
respectively; they had the greatest capacity of
all the railcars seating 43 people each.
[Photo: J.G. Dewing]

The original petrol railcar No. 1 and trailer at Stranorlar East on 15th July, 1931. This little four wheeled railcar had been bought as early as 1907 from Alldays and Onions of Birmingham, originally powered by a 10 hp petrol engine and capable of carrying 10 people. It was principally used as a convenient service vehicle and for post office mails, but also for passenger traffic on occasion. Henry Forbes, Traffic Superintendent of the line introduced railcars to the line as early as 1926 and there is little doubt that, at the end of the day, these saved the passenger service, if not the railway, for this was cut off by the Free State border from its original and convenient source of supplies. So successful was this policy that Mr Forbes converted and operating loss into a net receipt of £25,000, equal to 25% of the gross receipts. [Photo: A.W. Croughton]

Railcar No. 12 at Strabane with a box van in tow. This railcar was delivered in 1934 and set the pattern for the rest of the fleet. It was the first railcar supplied by Walkers of Wigan and combined a Walkers' diesel engine power bogie fitted with a Gardner 6L1 diesel engine and a body built by the GNR at Dundalk. A similar vehicle had been supplied two years earlier to the Clogher Valley Railway and Henry Forbes then sat on the CVR's Committee of Management and quick on the uptake to develop the concept for the CDRJC. [Photo: P.B. Whitehouse]

Railcar No. 12 at Rossnowlagh in May, 1949 with a Ballyshannon bound train including two goods vans with the rear one being loaded up from the platform. Note the railcar bonnet covers are both lifted up to enable air to cool the engine. After the Second World War, it became essential to keep running costs to a minimum, especially the high costs of steam locomotive usage; and so goods wagons were often attached to the passenger railcar services where possible. [Photo: P.B. Whitehouse]

Gardner engined Railcars No's 14 and 10 inside the trainshed at Killybegs station in 1958. These railcars proved very light on the permanent way which also aided the railway's longevity.

Railcar No. 8 (O'Doherty type) at Donegal in June, 1949. Railcars No's 7 & 8 were identical and became the first diesel railcars ever to run in regular service in the British Isles. They had a 32 seat body and were powered by a Gardner engine. [Photo: P.B. Whitehouse]

Former Clogher Valley Railway railcar No. 10 hauling two open wagons passes through Lough Eske station with a Stranorlar bound service. On the closure of the CVR this railcar was bought by the CDRJC to become No. 10 in its fleet. It retained its 28 seat body making it the smallest of the railcars used in later years. It has since been preserved at the Northern Ireland Cultra museum. [Photo: P.B. Whitehouse]

Walker railcar No. 18 entering Strabane. It was built in 1936, articulated and powered by a Gardner 6LW engine of 102 bhp and carried up to 41 passengers.

O'Doherty railcar No. 6, converted into a trailer car in October 1945 when its 6 litre petrol engine was removed.

Railcar No. 10 hauling trailer car and box van near Lough Eske with a Strabane-Donegal-Killybegs service in 1957. The longest section on the Donegal main line was from Stranorlar to Lough Eske. [Photo: P.B. Whitehouse]

Victoria Bridge station, Londonderry. [Photo: P.B. Whitehouse]

Right: The up starting signal at Donegal station showing distinct signs of Midland Railway parentage. On the extreme right is the signal box controlling the entrance and exit to the east with a trident signal shown beyond and to the left of the starting signal; to its left is the advance starting signal whilst the Ballyshannon branch comes in from the right. [Photo: P.B. Whitehouse]

Donegal couplings.

CDJRC container No. 1 sits in open wagon No. 108 built in 1893. These containers were sealed by customs and so could be taken through from Northern Ireland to the Republic.

Credit must be given to Henry Forbes, Traffic Superintendent of the line, for his painstaking instructions. Every copy of the Working Time Table and the bulkier red bound appendix carried the message: '*REMEMBER! It is well for each Member of this Railway to bear in mind that goodwill based upon years of conscientious effort may be entirely destroyed by a moment's indifference toward a customer.*'

No. 101 ISSUE.

THE
COUNTY DONEGAL RAILWAYS
(JOINT COMMITTEE.)

WORKING TIME TABLE

(For use of Committee's Staff only)

AS

From SUNDAY, 29th JUNE, 1958

until further notice.

M—Rail Car Service.   S—Steam Train.

No Special Train, Engine or Motor must be allowed to run over the Line without authority from the Manager's Office, and before any such Special is despatched, the Station Masters concerned must see that complete arrangements are made for its safe working, and that of any other Train or Trains which it may have to precede, cross or follow. Station Masters must see that the E.T.S. arrangements and signalling of Trains are carried out, and that a copy of the Special Train Notice is sent to gatekeepers under their supervision. A single bar thus — denotes the station appointed for a train to cross another travelling in the opposite direction.

REMEMBER !

It is well for each Member of this Railway to bear in mind that goodwill based upon years of conscientious effort may be entirely destroyed by a moment's carelessness or indifference toward a customer.

An early Austin 7 saloon car is transported by rail in single plank dropsided wagon No. 254 (which has been converted from a covered transship wagon).

Irish Narrow Gauge Album

Giant's Causeway, Portrush & Bush Valley Railway & Tramway Company Limited steam tram and train. The line connected Bushmills to Portrush in north Antrim and became the first serious application of electric traction in the British Isles. Although the Volks Electric Railway in Brighton was actually the first railway, it was only ¼ mile long. The railway was not permitted to lay an electric conductor third rail in the streets of either town and so steam trams were purchased for this work and the anticipated goods traffic. The tramway suffered from electricity leakage and so the steam trams ended up doing the bulk of the haulage. The tramway carried several hundreds of thousands of passengers to the famous basalt rock formations at the Giant's Causeway, which remain one of Ireland's foremost tourist attractions.

Chapter Fourteen

The Giant's Causeway Tram
George Behrend

We drove to Portrush to see the Giant's Causeway Tram. It was only eight miles or so long; so the trams ran frequently, as trams should; roughly every 15 minutes or more. And it was a proper tram. Moreover it was not a single car, but a single deck tram hauling a trailer. Soon it was time for the tram to leave. Its driver signalled to us to get aboard, so we dodged across the road among the few motor cars and many donkey carts and pony traps. This side of the trailer was quite open, with a running board all along the side, and grab handles to heave yourself in by. We settled for the trailer car, in preference to the stuffy tramcar, on whose open end platforms only the driver and conductor might stand. It started off, like trams anywhere, along the side of the road. Outside Portrush, it settled on the verge, brushed by a hedge most of the way which was why the doors were on one side only. No one wanted the brambles in their faces. Beyond the hedge lay some fields, then the sea.

Tram No. 3 *Dunluce Castle,* delivered in 1886 by Wilkinsons who supplied all the four locomotives on the line seen on 15th July, 1933. These tram locos were single manned and could only be fired in one direction when running. [Photo: A.W. Croughton]

Tram and trainers swayed, as 4 wheelers do, on indifferent track. The trolley jumped off the wire as we went over the run round loop points at Portrush, but the conductor was ready for this, and had the pole back up on the wire again so quickly that the driver barely noticed. Another tram was approaching the other way, and the conductor took advantage of the pause to transfer himself to the trailer before it arrived. Then we set off again, the conductor clambering along the running board, and hooking his arm around roof stanchions, to leave both hands free for issuing tickets. The lurching was chronic, the conductor slow, anyone less experienced would undoubtedly have been thrown off.

A violent banging on the gong sent the conductor scurrying along the footboard as the tram slowed down, then the conductor jumped rather acrobatically onto the tram's step, and I noticed that the pole was waving in the air again. This time, he was not nearly so adroit, as he missed the wire – more clanging on the gong, as the driver furiously wound the hand brake to stop the tram running backwards. It was clear the tram objected as much as the driver stopping on a

The open car is fully loaded on the tram as it passes Dunluce Castle. Note the power rail on the far side of the tram, before the overhead system was installed.

hill, requiring careful twiddling of the handles to get it going again without damaging the motors. Shortly afterwards we stopped docilely in another loop for no apparent reason, and the conductor finished collecting his fares.

Presently another tram came from round the corner out of sight; the corners were hidden by hills. The tram drivers had no signals, yet at the next loop here was another tram waiting for us. The loop was round another corner and we whizzed by at top speed. It appeared to be Irish magic. By now the conductor had taken the fares and spent the rest of the way to Bushmills nursing the pole, which frequently de-wired. We

clattered through another loop, then round another corner and here was Bushmills distillery and tram depot.

The tram now did a U-turn to the left, the depot fan being on the right, a straight run in from Portrush. Now the tram bounded across country making for the coast. The track ran much straighter than beside the sinewy road and then ended in what appeared to be the middle of nowhere. A track led round a bluff, and beyond was the famous Causeway with its hexagonal rock formation. The tram was infinitely more enticing than the Causeway. Even in 1939 we could say 'they don't have electric trams like this anymore!'

The open car is fully loaded on the tram as it passes Dunluce Castle.

Two views of the electric tram at the Causeway Hotel.

The electric tram with two trailers head for Bushmills as it runs round Methody Corner at the junction of Main and Causeway Streets and past the war memorial in Portrush . The last car, No. 18, is a seven bench toastrack trailer seating 28 passengers which was acquired in 1897. By 1899, overhead electric wires had been installed in place of the third rail, after a cyclist died following contact with it.

Irish Railways: Report of the Commissioners

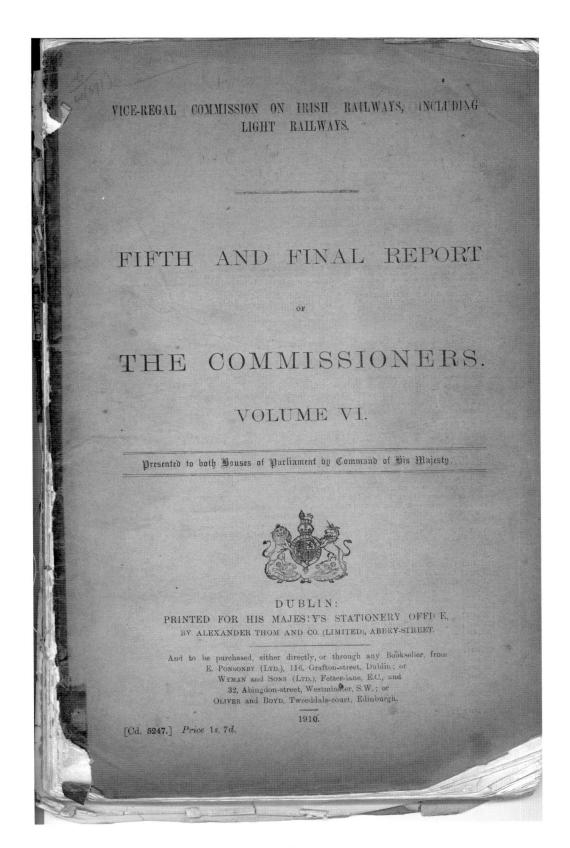

VICE-REGAL COMMISSION ON IRISH RAILWAYS, INCLUDING LIGHT RAILWAYS.

FIFTH AND FINAL REPORT

OF

THE COMMISSIONERS.

VOLUME VI.

Presented to both Houses of Parliament by Command of His Majesty.

DUBLIN:
PRINTED FOR HIS MAJESTY'S STATIONERY OFFICE,
BY ALEXANDER THOM AND CO. (LIMITED), ABBEY-STREET.

And to be purchased, either directly, or through any Bookseller, from
E. PONSONBY (LTD.), 116, Grafton-street, Dublin; or
WYMAN and SONS (LTD.), Fetter-lane, E.C., and
32, Abingdon-street, Westminster, S.W.; or
OLIVER and BOYD, Tweeddale-court, Edinburgh.

1910.

[Cd. 5247.]   Price 1s. 7d.

XXXVIII.—Summary of Principal Recommendations.

251. We have now, in pursuance of Your Excellency's Warrant, set forth the results of our Inquiry into the present working of Railways in Ireland. Our principal Recommendations on the question of their future working we summarise as follows :—

I. That an Irish Authority be instituted to acquire the Irish Railways and work them as a single system.

II. That this Authority be a Railway Board of twenty Directors, four nominated, and sixteen elected.

III. That the general terms of purchase be those prescribed by the Regulation of Railways Act of 1844 (7 & 8 Vic., cap. 85, sec. 2), with supplementary provisions as to redemption of guarantees, and purchase of non-dividend paying or non-profit earning lines.

IV. That the financial medium be a Railway Stock ; and that such Stock be charged upon (1) the Consolidated Fund ; (2) the net revenues of the unified Railway system ; (3) an annual grant from the Imperial Exchequer ; and (4) a general rate, to be struck by the Irish Railway Authority if and when required.

252. In conclusion, we have pleasure in recording that our necessarily long and complicated Inquiry has been much facilitated, at every stage of its progress, by the efficiency of our Secretary, Mr. George E. Shanahan, and his unremitting interest in the object of our proceedings. Not alone have all the duties pertaining to his office been discharged with marked ability, courtesy, and tact, but his special knowledge of the subject referred to us for investigation has enabled him to render exceptional assistance to every member of the Commission, entitling him thereby to our warm recognition, and constituting a public service of distinguished merit and we hope of lasting value.

We have the honour to be,

Your Excellency's obedient Servants,

CHARLES SCOTTER,
Chairman.

PIRRIE,

W. HUTCHESON POË,

THOMAS SEXTON.

GEORGE E. SHANAHAN,
Secretary,

13, St. Stephen's Green, N.,
Dublin,

VICE-REGAL COMMISSION UNDER HIS EXCELLENCY'S SIGN MANUAL.

DUBLIN CASTLE,
July 19, 1906.

The Lord Lieutenant has been pleased to issue a Commission to the following effect :—

BY THE LORD LIEUTENANT GENERAL AND GENERAL GOVERNOR OF IRELAND.

ABERDEEN.

WHEREAS it is deemed expedient that a Commission should issue to inquire into the present working of Railways in Ireland, including Light Railways, and to report how far they afford, separately or in conjunction with other means of transit, adequate facilities for the cheap and rapid transport of goods and passengers within the island and to Great Britain; what causes have retarded the expansion of traffic upon the Irish lines and their full utilisation for the development of the agricultural and industrial resources of the country; and, generally, by what methods the economical, efficient, and harmonious working of the Irish Railways can best be secured :

Now We, John Campbell, Earl of Aberdeen, Lord Lieutenant General and General Governor of Ireland, do hereby nominate, constitute, and appoint you, Sir Charles Scotter, Chairman of the London and South-Western Railway (Chairman); the Right Honourable William James Pirrie, Chairman of Harland and Wolff, Limited, Shipbuilders and Engineers; Sir Herbert Jekyll, Knight Commander of the Most Distinguished Order of St. Michael and St. George, an Assistant Secretary of the Board of Trade; Lieutenant-Colonel William Hutcheson Poë, Companion of the Most Honourable Order of the Bath; Thomas Sexton, Esquire; William Mitchell Acworth, Esquire; and John Audley Frederick Aspinall, Esquire, General Manager of the Lancashire and Yorkshire Railway, to be Commissioners for the purpose aforesaid.

And for the better effecting the purpose of this Our Commission, We do by these presents authorise and empower you, or any two or more of you to be named by you, to call before you or any two or more of you, to be so named, such persons as you may think fit to examine, and by whom you may be the better informed of the matter hereby submitted for your consideration and everything connected therewith, and generally to inquire of and concerning the premises by all other lawful ways and means whatsoever. And also to call for and examine such books, papers, documents, writings, or records, as you or any two or more of you as aforesaid shall think useful for the purpose of the inquiry.

And We also by these presents authorise and empower you, or any two or more of you as aforesaid, to visit and personally inspect such places as you, or any two or more of you, may deem expedient for the purpose aforesaid. And Our pleasure is that you, or any two or more of you as aforesaid, do from time to time and with all convenient speed report to Us what you shall find touching and concerning the premises.

And We further by these presents ordain that this Our Commission shall continue in full force and virtue, and that you, Our Commissioners, do from time to time proceed in the execution thereof, although the same not be continued from time to time by adjournment.

And We do hereby appoint George E. Shanahan, Esquire, the Assistant Secretary to the Commissioners of Public Works in Ireland, to be the Secretary of this Our Commission.

Given at His Majesty's Castle at Dublin, this 18th day of July, 1906.

By His Excellency's Command.
J. B. DOUGHERTY.

The Commission, at its first sitting, adopted the short title of :—
THE VICE-REGAL COMMISSION ON IRISH RAILWAYS.

XXXV.—The Victoria Bridge and Castlederg Tramway.

Davidson, 54604-10.

215. Towards the close of our Inquiry, our attention was called to the unfortunate position of a tramway 7¾ miles in length laid on the public road between Victoria Bridge, on the Great Northern Railway and Castlederg. The line was authorised by a special Act of Parliament passed a few months before the introduction of the Tramways Act of 1883. The authorised share capital is £20,000, of which £13,000 was issued under a 5 per cent. guarantee given by the baronies of Upper Strabane, Lower Strabane, and West Omagh, for a period of thirty-five years expiring in July 1919. Of the balance of £7,000, the sum of £6,080 was provided by the issue of ordinary shares, and in addition a sum of £5,500 was raised by mortgage of the undertaking at 4 per cent. The total share and loan capital issued, amounting in all to £24,580, has not been quite sufficient to meet the cost of construction and rolling stock equipment, and a sum of £541 remains as a debt on capital account.

Appendix 10, Final Report.

Davidson, 54626, 54643.

54675.

216. The line has been fairly successful, but the district is purely agricultural, and although traffic has made a substantial growth, the maximum liability in respect of the guarantee has always had to be made good. A return handed in by the Secretary of the company shows that for the three years ending on 30th June, 1909, the receipts averaged £6 14s. 11d. per mile per week, and the expenditure £5 5s. 3d. The average annual profit in the same period was £598 10s. 3d. an amount little more than sufficient to pay interest on the mortgage, and on a bank overdraft, incurred some years ago to meet the cost of a new engine. The Secretary informed us that the line was short of rolling stock, and that a sum of about £6,400 was required, partly to meet this want, and partly for the improvement of the line, and for the provision of additional sidings and of a small workshop for minor repairs. He also stated that it had been in contemplation for some years to extend the tramway to Killeter, a distance of 5 miles, at an estimated cost of £25,000, but that there was no prospect in existing circumstances of raising the necessary capital.

54653.

217. Looking to the fact that this tramway owes its existence entirely to the people of the district; that it has so far received no assistance from the Government, such as similar lines projected a few months later, under the Act of 1883, enjoyed; and that present guaranteed shareholders will after 1919 be entirely dependent on the earnings of the line, we consider that this is a case in which a grant of £6,000 might properly and usefully be made.

Bogie carriage No. 5 in the last year of the C&VBT's operation in 1933. Note the wire mesh over the bogies. This carriage was built in 1887 by the Oldbury Railway Carriage & Wagon Co. [Photo: A.W. Croughton].

C&VBT cattle train pauses for the photographer alongside the roadway around 1924. Hudswell Clarke 2-6-0T No. 4 (works No. 698 built 1904) runs cab first and with parts of her tramway skirts removed for ease of access to motion oiling points. No. 4 was only fitted with protecting skirts on one side of the locomotive as the line ran only on the northern side of the roadway and the locomotive was never turned; it always faced chimney first towards Castlederg. [Photo: H.C. Casserley]

Heraldic device
[Photo: A.W. Croughton]

First/Third Class composite 4-wheeled carriage No. 2 with wire mesh along the entire underside. Also built by the English Oldbury firm but earlier in 1884 and originally designated First/Second composite, it was redesignated in 1887. [Photo: A.W. Croughton]

Title of Act under which constructed	RAILWAY	Mileage Broad	Mileage Narrow	Worked by	Share Capital Guaranteed £	Free Grant £	Treasury Liability Maximum £	Treasury Liability Average paid five years ending 1908 £	Average Baronial contributions for Dividends and Deficits five years ending 1908 £	Date of opening of line
Tramways (Ireland) Act, 1883.	1. Schull and Skibbereen	—	14½	Committee of Management of County Council	57,000	—	1,140	1,140	3,021	1886
	2. Clogher Valley	—	37	Owning Company	123,310	—	2,466	2,453	4,097	1887
	3. West Clare	—	27	Do.	163,500	—	3,270	2,733	3,444	1887
	4. Cork and Muskerry	—	18	Do.	75,500	—	1,500	817	817	1887-8
	5. Cavan and Leitrim	—	48½	Do.	190,585	—	3,811	3,662	5,446	1887-8
	6. Carrickfergus Harbour Junction	1	—	Midland (Northern Counties Committee)	6,500	—	130 (a)	— (a)	375	1887-8
	7. Dublin and Blessington	15½	—	Owning Company	40,000	—	800	581	790	1888
	8. West Donegal	—	4	County Donegal Railways Joint Committee	17,000	—	340 (b)	261 (to date of redemption 1889.)	448 (c) (to date of last payment in 1900.)	1889
	9. Loughrea and Attymon	9	—	Midland Great Western Company	54,445	—	1,089	820	820	1890
	10. Mitchelstown and Fermoy	12	—	Great Southern and Western Company	60,000	—	1,200 (d)	1,115 (to date of redemption 1900.)	800 (e)	1891
	11. Timoleague and Courtmacsherry	9	—	Committee of Management of County Council	35,000	—	700	700 (to date of redemption 1888.)	1,774	1890-1
	12. Tralee and Dingle	—	37½	Do.	120,000	—	2,400 (f)	2,400	5,975	1891
Light Railways (Ireland) Act, 1889.	13. Ballinrobe and Claremorris	12	—	Midland Great Western Company	71,640	—	1,433	1,075	1,075	1892
	14. South Clare	—	26	West Clare Company	120,000	—	2,400	2,288	3,196	1892
	15. Donoughmore Extension	—	8½	Cork and Muskerry Company	30,000	—	600	600	932	1893
	16. Tuam and Claremorris	17	—	Great Southern and Western Company	98,000	—	1,960	772 (g)	— (g)	1894
	17. Headford and Kenmare	19¾	—	Do.	60,000	49,984	1,200	1,200	1,200	1893
	18. Killorglin and Valentia	26¾	—	Do.	70,000	85,000	1,400	1,400	1,400	1893
	19. Donegal and Killybegs	—	19	County Donegal Railways Joint Committee	1,000	121,436	20 (h)	11 (to date of cancellation in 1906)	153 (i)	1893
	20. Stranorlar and Glenties	—	24½	Do.	1,000	123,886	20 (j)	Nil. (to date of cancellation in 1906)	Nil. (k)	1895
	21. Colloney and Swinford	29½	—	Great Southern and Western Company	80,000	} 146,042	1,600	200	87	1895
Railways (Ireland) Act, 1896.	22. Claremorris and Swinford	18	—	Do.	40,000	}	800	287	287	1895
	23. Bantry Bay Extension	2	—	Cork, Bandon and South Coast Company	—	14,940	—	—	—	1892
	24. Ardglass Extension	8	—	Belfast and County Down Company	—	29,980	—	—	—	1893
	25. Ballina and Killala	8	—	Midland Great Western Company	—	44,000	—	—	—	1893
	26. Skibbereen and Baltimore	7½	—	Cork, Bandon and South Coast Company	—	56,700	—	—	—	1893
	27. Westport and Mallaranny	18	—	Midland Great Western Company	—	131,400	—	—	—	1894
	28. Galway and Clifden	49¼	—	Do.	—	264,600	—	—	—	1895
	29. Achill Extension	8¼	—	Do.	—	72,578	—	—	—	1895
	30. Buncrana and Carndonagh	—	18½	Londonderry and Lough Swilly Company	—	98,527	—	—	—	1901
	31. Letterkenny and Burtonport	—	49½	Do.	—	313,648	—	—	—	1903
	Totals	270½	332½		£1,513,980	£1,552,721 (l)	£30,279	(m) £24,515	(n) £36,137	

Broad + Narrow = 603

(a). As the line has not been opened for passenger traffic, the Treasury has no liability.

(b) (d) (f). Treasury liability redeemed under the Tramways (Ireland) Act, 1895.

(c) (i) (k). Baronial liability extinguished under the Great Northern (Ireland) and Midland Railways Act, 1906.

(e). Fixed payment under the Great Southern and Western Company's Act, 1900. This liability will be extinguished on 30th June, 1910.

(g). Guaranteeing area indemnified against liability under the Great Southern and Western Company's Amalgamation Act, 1900.

(h) (j). Treasury liability extinguished under the Great Northern (Ireland) and Midland Railways Act, 1906.

(l). Exclusive of £7,321 for preliminary expenses.

(m). Less £3,787 no longer payable in respect of (b) (d) (f) (h) (j).

(n). Less £601, no longer payable in respect of (c) & (i).